A Vase for a Flower

A VASE FOR A FLOWER

Tales of an Antique Dealer

by
Denny Pinkus
With illustrations by Shlomo Zafrir

ST. MARTIN'S PRESS
New York

Library of Congress Cataloging-in-Publication Data

Pinkus, Denny.
　　A vase for a flower: tales of an antique dealer / Denny Pinkus.
　　　　p.　　cm.
　　ISBN 0-312-04258-2
　　1. Israel—Social life and customs.　2. Pinkus, Denny.　3. Antique
dealers—Israel—Biography.　I. Title.
DS112.P63　1990
956.9405—dc20　　　　　　　　　　　　　　　　　　　　89-70319
　　　　　　　　　　　　　　　　　　　　　　　　　　　　　CIP

First published in Great Britain by George Weidenfeld and Nicolson Limited
under the title *Antique Dealer*.

First U.S. Edition
10 9 8 7 6 5 4 3 2 1

To Nurit, Erela, Ron, Liat and Dana –
my family

If you close your eyes at sunrise . . .
. . . you cannot see the stars at night.

Contents

Foreword

With all those stories, why don't you write a book? That was the question people asked me. I never knew what to answer. Maybe I did not have the right pen, or maybe the right notebook. I had a typewriter, but I did not like it. I tried once, and even wrote five pages. It was not it. So I started to dream to have my own computer. After many dreams, I bought my computer. I did not even know how to press a key. The day I learned to press my first key was the day that I wrote my first letter of this book. After seven weeks the book was ready. What now?

I want to express my gratitude to David Hinden, who had the patience to read every word of my book and correct it in such a way that you won't find out that English is not my mother tongue. Though he left my expressions that are not known as proper English, with the excuse of literary freedom – or whatever it is called.

I asked my friend, the artist Shlomo Zafrir, to make some drawings of the people, or at least their type, to whom these stories belong. We created them together.

Some of these stories are true. Some of them are so fantastically unbelievable that they must be true.

I want to thank all those collectors, all those crazy people who bring colour into life. Their success and their failures made this book possible.

The day I held my first antiquity in my hands, I had a wonderful feeling. I felt that I was holding history, and it was mine.

Today, after forty years, and the thousands of objects that my hands have held, I still have the same feeling.

Denny Pinkus

The Violin

Freud said that a collector is actually a person who as a child did not receive enough love, so he has to surround himself with objects that will keep him warm. Objects that he loves – and he thinks that the objects love him.

An antique dealer is actually a collector, a frustrated collector. He sells the goods that he has collected. I am an antique dealer.

Any ordinary man gets up in the morning, puts his coat on and goes to work. It is as if his coat is second nature to him. A personality. When he gets home in the evening, he takes off his coat and becomes a different person. I wear my coat all the time. Here, at work, and at home. Day and night.

Antiques are not just objects. Antiques are life itself. Antiques are drama, history, even misery. Sometimes even life and death. Yes.

There are people who talk to plants, I talk to my antiques. Sometimes the stories sound like fantasy, like fairytales. Sometimes even I have trouble believing they really happened. One morning an elderly woman – well, you can say old – came into the gallery. She was holding a package wrapped in a towel. She was about seventy: short, clean and tidy, and very simply dressed. She was wearing a small black hat with a tulle veil, plain black-laced shoes with a small heel. She was holding a bag, the handle of which was so long that the bag trailed on the ground. In her other hand she was holding, as if it were an infant, a package wrapped in a towel, tied with a lot of string. The woman entered

11

5 Zafrin. 88.

the gallery hesitantly. She stopped just inside the doorway. She looked over the premises; her lack of self-confidence was clearly evident. She looked around and was silent.

I momentarily stopped polishing an antique Damascus table. I raised my eyes and looked at her. I scrutinized her. She scrutinized me. A few seconds of silence. Then, 'Are you the owner?' I nodded.

'Brought you a violin.'

'I don't sell violins!'

'I know.'

She crossed cautiously to the table where I was seated and laid the package on the table. She undid the strings binding the parcel and removed an old violin and a bow. She lifted them with both hands. She showed them to me, like a mother displaying her baby. I examined both the woman and the violin with increasing interest. There was something mystical about this woman; something which could not be explained.

'Sit down,' I said. She did not sit.

'This is a very special violin. Little children played it about seventy years ago in Safed. Do you understand?' She shook her finger at me. I took the violin and examined it.

'Why did you come to me?'

'I have already been to all the antique dealers in town and no one wanted to buy it. You are the last.'

I knew there was something. I can't explain it, but immediately I felt that there was a real story here. A tale straight out of the storybook of life. The woman. The violin wrapped in a towel. All the antique dealers had turned her away. I was filled with great excitement. I felt her honesty go right to my heart. She spoke to me. I believed her. I also saw a little label inside the violin, that meant nothing to me. I only can say that the label was born with the violin. But, what do I have to do with violins?

The woman raised her little finger: 'Do you understand? It is not any old violin . . . do you understand?'

'How much do you want for it?'

'I need only five thousand, that is all.'

'Why five thousand?'

'Because that's how much I need to get into an old-people's home, where I can live out the rest of my days in dignity. This violin is all I possess. I have kept it for a long time. For many years. I am childless. I have no one. Listen, please, you don't have to pay it all at once. Each time you'll have to pay a little. When you have it . . .'

I made up my mind.

Old Jaffa is the oldest port in the world. It is built all in stone in the oriental way. Beautiful. The old lady and I walked together down an Old Jaffa alley and I started thinking, 'Now I have a violin . . .'

That very same day I took her to an old-people's home. 'There'll be a vacancy in three months,' they told me. I deal in antiquities that are thousands of years old. What is three months?

On the table in the back room were the violin and bow. I hovered over them, as if considering how to begin handling my new acquisition. From the nearby book case I took a book on antique musical instruments. I leafed through the book, but did not find anything to link my violin to the pictures in the technical book. Now I sat on the chair and stared at the violin, as if looking for something hidden. It was as if I was trying to get the violin to tell me its story. That the violin was no Stradivarius I saw at once. I can identify antiques even from a distance. Antiques, but not violins.

The whole night I sat up looking for a mark which would identify my violin. At four o'clock in the morning, when I was more asleep than awake, I discovered, on the underside of the violin, an inscription which, for some reason, had escaped my sight until that moment. Roggieri, it said. Roggieri.

I had no trouble finding out from my books that Roggieri was one of the greatest Italian violin-makers of the early eighteenth century. He had studied violin-making together with Stradivarius. For the first time since I bought my fiddle, I knew that I was the owner of an object of great value, of great importance.

Miriam had a little coffee shop next door. She thought that she was my mother – or something like that. She always protected me, and always had a coffee ready when a customer visited my gallery. She had to know everything and I did not care. Miriam saw my violin and every day she used to come and see what I was doing, or even if I had started to play. Miriam is a heavy woman with black hair, wearing a cheap dress with a floral print. Her generous bosom is always partly exposed. She tries to arrange her dress every few minutes. She wears, most of the time, wooden clogs which make a noise when she walks.

She entered the gallery holding a tray with a small cup of coffee and a tall glass of water. She saw me standing, holding the violin. She was amused and burst into laughter.

'Do you like it, Miriam?'

'It's a violin like any other. What are you going to do with it? Start playing?'

'Maybe ... who knows?'

'Drink your coffee. It'll get cold.'

'Thank you, Miriam.'

When she saw she was not getting my attention, she felt superfluous. She crossed to the doorway and left. On her way out she said, 'Fiddler on the roof'. She could hardly refrain from laughing.

Sheinkin Street in Tel-Aviv. Just another old street in the city. There was a coffee shop where dealers, antique dealers, used to meet. From two until four in the afternoon. This was the place where dealers used to buy antiques or trade among themselves.

Three dealers were sitting at table one. There were only three tables, but each one had a number. I still don't know why. Puchachevsky, old Isser (the Ganev) and Berger. They were bored, maybe waiting for customers. They talked. Then I approached from the corner, the violin tucked under my arm. I still had it wrapped in the same towel. The three dealers recognized the violin, and suddenly everything came to life.

'So, you bought it? Some dealer!'

'A real connoisseur of violins, you can be sure of it. An expert. A big expert.'

Berger took off his hat and threw it to the ground and, pretending to be a street musician, he began to sing, 'If I were a rich man ...' Isser took out a few coins and threw them into the hat. All three laughed loudly. I sat down on one of the empty chairs. Berger poured some coffee into a china cup for me and said, 'Come on, show us the great find. Please teach us your expert eye.'

'You have seen it already, long before I did ...'

'Indeed we have.' They all burst out laughing. I just smiled.

At breakfast my wife sat beside me. She was preparing a meal.

15

'Five thousand? Peanuts! Do you know what we could have done with that money? Do you?'

'It is an original Roggieri. There are only a few of them in the world. The old woman was right! She knew what she was talking about.'

'I beg your pardon, but Roggieri means nothing to me! And I couldn't care less. When we wanted to buy me a car, you said there was no money, so how come there's money for the fiddle?'

'The old woman was right. She said "You'll make a lot of money . . . little children played it seventy years ago in Safed." I don't know how much it is worth. I'm going to London.'

I found Mr Mackenzie's shop without any trouble. Mackenzie was a world-renowned violin assessor. He did not say a word. He had my violin in his hands. When I saw his pupils dilate, I remembered an old Chinese proverb: 'When a dealer's pupils dilate, he is looking at something that's valuable. When the pupils contract, the object is of no interest.' Mackenzie's pupils were enormous.

'How much can I get for it?'

'Whatever you ask. Where is its box?'

I was looking for her address. I found it.

'Tea's ready. Shall I pour you a cup?' My old lady looked a little worried. She was afraid something had happened and the deal was off. 'Has anything happened?'

'Yes, two things happened. Firstly, I've been notified by the old-people's home that your room is ready, and, about the violin, it is an original Roggieri from the year 1711. I think we'll make a lot of money.'

'I told you, I told you, children played it in Safed seventy years ago . . .'

'Tell me, Madam Rosa, the case – where is the box the violin was in?'

'I remember . . . there was a box. It had paintings, no . . . no paintings but wooden engravings on it. It was very pretty. It was brown. It wasn't used because the handle was a little broken. I don't know who has it. I was a child. It was a long time ago. Many children played it, many, but . . . who was the last one? I can't remember. Go to Safed, they'll be sure to know.'

To find a case in a city is crazy. To try to do it is insane. Now I was in Safed and I started to ask old people if they knew anything about a case for a violin. I got only negative answers. I said to myself, listen old fellow, give up. I did almost give up hope.

I was on my way to my old car, when I saw him. He was sitting at the entrance to his house, completely still. A very old man of about eighty years old, white-bearded, sitting on a tin, on a balcony, overlooking Safed and the Galilee. The man looked like a statue. 'Shalom'. The man did not answer, did not move. 'It's a beautiful day today'. The man did not move. 'They say it'll be beautiful tomorrow as well.' No response. 'Have you been living here for many years?' No answer. 'Rosa has sent me to you.'

For the first time the old man looked at me. The name Rosa had struck a chord. 'She said maybe you could help me. I'm looking for a child, or rather, somebody who was a child seventy years ago and played the violin. This violin.'

The old man came to life. He lowered his eyes to the violin. I handed him the violin. The old man reached out and took the violin in both hands. He turned it over and broke into a smile, as if he were remembering things from his childhood. I was moved. The man placed the violin on his left shoulder and looked at the bow in his right hand. He got up and walked to the edge of the balcony. The old man laid the bow on the strings and began to play. I was enchanted by the music. Jewish music.

People in Safed tell a story that a crazy man was running through the narrow streets of Safed, showing a wooden box of a violin and dancing all the way down to his old car. There are even some who will swear to God that they saw the real fiddler on the roof.

My finger was on the telephone dial. 'I'd like to speak to Maestro Anatoli Nehemkin.'

'Yes?'

'My name is Pinkus and I have an original Roggieri for sale. If you are interested please come to my gallery in Old Jaffa.'

Nehemkin came in. He looked indifferent, but at the same time it was clear that he was most excited. Anatoli took the violin and started to play. He closed his eyes and was greatly moved. He began to play a virtuoso piece, Paganini Number One. Just for me. He finished and I applauded enthusiastically. 'How much do you ask for it?'

'What is it worth to you?' a brief pause.

'Twenty thousand.' I shook my head without a moment's reflection. Nehemkin crossed to the opening between the two rooms. He took a step as if he was about to leave. He came back to the opening and said, 'Twenty-five thousand! Take it or leave it!' I shook my head again – and it meant the answer was no.

I was in London again. I took a seat. The auctioneer declared, 'Lot number 151, original Roggieri violin. Year 1711. Starting fifty thousand . . .' A pretty hostess displayed my violin to the audience. The gavel fell. 'Going, for the first time . . . going for the second . . . gone!' My violin was sold for one hundred thousand. Who was the buyer? Anatoli Nehemkin.

The home was nice. When I entered I saw nice old ladies and smiling old gentlemen. I found Rosa: 'You see . . . that's all. That is the story of the violin. Now, half of the money is yours. Now you can buy whatever you want.'

She placed her hand on my shoulder, like a much more experienced person, and said, 'Do you remember? I promised you'd make a lot of money on this violin. Do you know why? Because little children played it seventy years ago in Safed. I don't need any money. Just promise me that after I am gone you will place a tombstone on my grave . . . and maybe say *Kaddish*. That is all I ask.'

I kept my promise.

The Rimonim

Among the Torah silver ornaments, the head pieces, *rimonim*, seem to be the oldest. *Rimonim* is the Hebrew word for pomegranates, a symbol of fertility and life. The two pillars of the Torah represent the pillars of the temple of King Solomon which were ornamented with pomegranates. 'A golden bell and a pomegranate, upon the skirts of the robe round about' (Exodus, 28.34). Herein undoubtedly lies the origin of the bells which are to be found on most of the *rimonim*. Pomegranates were also on the robe of the high priest, as quoted above from the Holy Bible.

Wherever Jews settled, the synagogue was the most important spiritual centre. After the destruction of the second temple, in the year 70 CE, the Jews' longing for the temple grew even more profound. The customs and traditions that crystallized in that period have been preserved, and in broad outline the entire Jewish people adheres to them to this day. Traditionally, the objects used for religious observance are divided into two categories: 'holy vessels' and 'ritual utensils'. Holy vessels are the *rimonim*. Yes, you need two *rimonim* for the Torah.

Wintertime in Old Jaffa, Israel, is sometimes quite cold. It was early evening when a man in his fifties came into my gallery, the Antiquarium. Among the items of silver that he offered for sale was one big *rimon*. Only one? 'You see, I don't want much for it. I kept it for so many years ... since I was a child. I was born in Germany. It was *Kristallnacht** and we all had to run to the

---

* The night of 10 November 1938 when the synagogues were burnt.

19

synagogue in order to save something. I was a little boy then. An old man opened the Torah shrine and handed to me this *rimon*** and said to me, "Run!" So I did. Then I was taken by a Christian family. I did not see my family again. Then we passed to the east, to Rumania. That's where I come from now. I am a newcomer to Israel and I need the money. I still remember our synagogue in Germany, it was beautiful ... You see, the Jews managed to remove and bury many Jewish objects, and that was before the Nazis bombed down and destroyed our beautiful synagogue.'

I had to be insane to buy only one *rimon*. It was of no use to a synagogue or to a collector of Judaica; the transaction was insane. But I did it, although I did not know why.

It was a beautiful silver *rimon*, decorated with crowns and bells and lions on top. Two-storey towers with alternating pierced windows and arches with bells. This *rimon* was made by a master, in the city of Fuerth, Germany, in the eighteenth century. So I had that *rimon*, I polished it and put it on display. Months passed and the *rimon* moved from one place to another. Again polishing, and again and again.

Years passed and this *rimon* always changed places. Here and there I had a collector who would ask about it and admire it. But always the same question: where is its pair?

One morning, after many years, I had a visit from a lady who wanted to sell antique silver objects. She opened her bag and I could not believe what my eyes saw. It was a dream. She had there the second *rimon*. I asked where did she get it, and she replied, 'I am a new immigrant from Argentina. I was born in Germany. It was the day, the terrible day, *Kristallnacht*, when the Nazis started to destroy the synagogues. We all ran to our synagogue, to save some of the things that were dear to our community. I ran, too. When I was next to the Torah ark I saw this *rimon* lying there. I took it, then when we got home I kept it with my dolls. I was sent to a convent. The nuns took care of me. Then after the war my father came back and found me. We left for Argentina. Now I am here.'

'Do you have any brothers or sisters?'

'Yes, I had a brother, but as far as I know he was killed in a concentration camp.'

---

* Silver pomegranate decorating Torah scrolls.

'How old was he?'

'He was three years older . . . I was three years younger . . .' She had tears in her eyes, me too. I bought all the silver she had, and after she went away I compared one *rimon* with the other. Everything, every detail, was exact. There was no mistake. The two *rimonim* were born together.

After a few weeks of research I found the man through the Jewish Agency and I asked the same questions again: 'Do you have any brothers and sisters?'

'Yes, I had a sister . . . she must be dead now, because I never heard from her.'

'How old was she?'

'She was three years younger, but why do you ask all these questions?'

Now I was sure: 'I know where your sister is. She is here in Israel. The *rimon* that you saved and the *rimon* that she saved are identical. I think you can meet your sister now.'

The man started shaking and sweating and did not know whether to laugh or cry. We went in my car to see his sister. It was his sister. A history of forty-four years passed in that room in seconds. You need two *rimonim* for the Torah. They are together now. Nothing can happen to them any more. They are in Israel. Brother and sister – the two *rimonim* for the Torah.

In the *Kristallnacht* the Nazis put a sign *'Jetzt kommt der liebe Mai und lass uns vom Juden frei'** on almost every synagogue in Germany. That was in 1938. But Jews have a better sign: *'Shemah Israel adonai eloheinu adonai achad'*.†

And that sign is three thousand four hundred years old. It has been ever since the Torah was given to Israel. The same Torah that in 1938 had two *rimonim* which are now safe in Israel.

---

* Now comes lovely May, to set us free from the Jews.
† Hear, O Israel, the Lord is our God, the Lord is One.

The Street Sweeper

Many, many years ago I had a little shop in Beer Sheba, the capital of the Negev. A town in the sands. It was just like having a shop in the middle of nowhere.

I loved the Bedouin market. The Bedouin used to come, and still do, every Wednesday in the afternoon to be ready for the market, Thursday morning at five thirty. I used to buy from them Bedouin hand-made bags; always fifty or sixty at a time. I bought them for three lira apiece, and sold them for five.

One Thursday morning I saw that the Bedouin were selling the same bags for three lira, the same price that I paid each week for fifty or sixty bags. I saw also that, if a tourist insisted, he could get it for less. I was mad at them. It was not fair, but I did not say a word. I waited.

The next week I hired ten students and dressed them as Bedouin. Every one had Bedouin bags for sale. When the real Bedouin started to sell their bags for three lira, I made a sign and my 'Bedouin' reduced the price to two and a half lira. The real Bedouin reduced the price to two lira. I made a sign again. My 'Bedouin' dropped the price to one and a half. One and a half – tourists went crazy. Nobody understood what was happening. The price went down to one lira, then a group of tourists invaded the market and bought all the bags, from all the Bedouin, the real and 'others'. These tourists were my 'tourists', another group of students that I hired for the job.

A week later the Bedouin sheiks came to my shop to invite me

22

for a *sulcha*. That was a party to make peace. We did. I was the man who put the price on the Bedouin bags, as long as I had them in stock.

I used to return from the Bedouin market at six o'clock in the morning. It was then that I saw him one day . . . He was an elderly man, very small. His broom was much bigger than he was. He had his little cart with two big cans to collect the dirt from the streets. He had a large straw hat, a very old one, and a plastic protector for his nose against sunburn. He was holding his broom while looking in my shop window. I had there a pottery wine pitcher from the period of King Solomon on display. He used to stand in front of it for several minutes. 'Shalom.' 'Shalom.' That was the extent of our conversation.

Every Thursday morning, the same thing happened. 'Shalom.' 'Shalom.' And that was all. I found that little man always looking at the same pitcher for many weeks. My curiosity started to grow and grow, until one day: 'Shalom, how are you this morning?'

'I am fine. How are you, sir?'

'Do you know what this pitcher is? And how old it is?'

'Yes.' He wanted to go away to continue his work. I did not let him go.

'Tell me.'

'It is from the Second Iron Age.' I thought that I was going to faint. If Professor Yigael Yadin would have given me that answer I would not have been surprised, but . . . a street sweeper? He walked away. But not before he said 'Shalom' and looked at his watch, as if he was in a hurry.

I entered my shop and went straight to my books. The man was right. It was Second Iron Age, the period of King David and King Solomon. I started talking to myself and I could not do anything that day. I was thrilled.

So, the next morning I got up early. I could not wait for next Thursday. It was raining and still I said to myself, the man is going to be there in front of my shop window. He was. Again standing and holding his broom in the same way, between his legs and holding himself to it.

'Shalom. Do you want that pitcher?'

'I would love to have it, but I know I cannot afford it. It must cost about three hundred and I don't have the money for it.'

'Can you afford five lira a month?'

'Yes, that I could, but who is going to give me a biblical pitcher for five a month. That would be crazy.'

'I am. Come in. We are going to prepare a document of sale. Every fifth of the new month you'll bring five lira and we write it down on your copy and on mine.'

The old man said yes, but did not believe what was going on. He entered the shop with his broom and wagon. I started to pack his pitcher in a box. The same as if I were selling it to the Prince of Wales. When the parcel was ready I gave it to him and he wrapped it with his coat and put it in the dirt can. This was the first time I saw the man smiling. I think we were both happy.

'Please tell me, how did you know the period so precisely? Please tell me.'

'I cannot tell you today, but I shall. You are a nice man. I'll tell you, but you will have to wait ... don't ask me why, I shall not explain. Thank you very much and *shalom*.'

The man left with his wagon, his broom and his King Solomon wine pitcher. Every fifth of the month he came and paid his five lira. It was like a Swiss clock. I wanted to ask him many times about my last question, but at the last moment I honoured what he had said to me: to wait.

Many months passed, and one morning when he came to pay his five lira I asked if he would like to have a cup of coffee with me. His answer was, 'Tea, please.' I put the water on to boil and when I had everything ready he started to talk.

'You see, I was born in Germany. I had a wife and three children. I was a teacher, I mean I was the professor of History and Archaeology at the Berlin University. I was taken by the Nazis to Auschwitz. My wife and children were killed before my eyes. They did not want to leave me, so they were shot. During my years in the concentration camp I used to work in the most terrible jobs. I used to collect the gold teeth of the dead Jews for the Nazis. I made a *neder*, a promise to God, that if I would come out alive from this hell I would come to the Holy Land to clean it. This is what I am doing.'

I don't know how long we were sitting there. My mouth was dry. The pain I felt was so big that I couldn't cry. I wanted to scream to the sky: 'Oh, God, do you see this, do you hear this ...?'

Rich Man, Poor Man

It was late evening. My daughter Erela and I were talking about her studies. Then he came in. It was just like a movie. Comic movie. A cowboy. A very short man, fat. He was wearing a very big cowboy hat, a very wide brass belt. Real high cowboy's boots. He also had a very large cigar. Those very large ones that actually need a light when you turn, just like a car, so as not to cause an accident. He stood in front of a showcase full of antiquities: Roman glass, pottery vases and urns, little Roman and Hellenistic statuettes, and so on. He stood like he was still on a Texan horse. He puffed his cigar every few minutes. Then without a word he went out, and came back after a few minutes. Again the same show. He did this about three times, and each time my daughter and I looked at one other without understanding a thing. Here he was again, with his big cigar, but this time he called me with his finger ...

I did not understand what he meant so I asked, 'Which item are you asking about, sir?'

'The whole case, everything, the case, the antiques, everything.'

'This is going to take at least one hour, I mean, to make the complete list of items, their period, and provenance, and the price.'

'Yes, you do that, but first let me call my wife.'

There she was. A very tall woman, about ten feet high and strongly built. When she talked to her husband, who called her

25

'honey', she called him 'honey'. My daughter and I wanted to laugh. But we did not.

'Do you like this, honey?'

'I love whatever you like.'

'OK. My dear fellow, you make your list. We are now going for a late dinner, and we'll be back in about one hour.'

My Erela opened her big eyes and said, 'Dad, you are not taking this comedy seriously.'

'I am. You sit down and write, while I am going to dictate about every antiquity. A customer has to be treated seriously.'

It was almost midnight, and Erela complained that her hand was hurting, but we finished. The short man with his big wife did not come. Erela had question-marks in her eyes, maybe I had too. We waited for twenty minutes and it was already late. We started to close the gallery, and here they came. Shorty and his big wife.

He came directly to the table, puffing a new big cigar. Without saying anything I showed him the list and the price. He went through the list very carefully. He took out his chequebook and wrote the big sum that was at the end of the list. His wife was happy. Then he took his camera, his polaroid, and photographed the showcase several times. He came back to me and said very seriously, 'You cash this cheque first, and then ship it all to me air cargo, to Texas.' He gave me his card. I wrote a receipt. I held the cheque for a very long time, until Erela took it from me. She did not believe what she was looking at.

I did not sleep all night. The next morning I went to my bank. I said to my bank manager, 'Listen to this unbelievable story.' I told him all . . . I don't know why he was not surprised. Maybe bankers should not be surprised. He looked at the cheque and read it several times.

'I don't think this is very funny, but to make sure why don't we send a cable to confirm it?' I agreed.

Two days later the manager called me on the phone: 'Your money is here, you can come now to pick it up.' It took me only a few minutes, and I was there. I did not believe it. I asked if I could write a cheque for a very big sum, and he answered 'Yes'. I wrote the cheque, and went to the teller. He had to open the safe for it. After ten minutes he gave me the pile of money. Immediately I deposited it again. I just wanted to see.

It took over two months to pack everything in special wooden boxes, to write certificates for every antiquity, to get an official export licence. I said a prayer, and shipped it all by plane.

Two weeks later the phone rang: 'Hi there. It's me, Harry . . . Yes, everything is OK, but . . . please tell me, was the green Roman bottle at the left or the right, in the showcase?'

I never saw my cowboy again. He was not a collector. He just wanted a creation. A complete piece of art. A showcase with antiquities found in the Holy Land – that was all.

5

I Had a Dream: the Talisman

Every Friday afternoon I work till about two o'clock. The whole week I wait for the *shabbat*. Friday afternoon tea is also my favourite meal. It gives me a wonderful feeling, because after that meal I go to sleep and get up only for the *kiddush*. That is something very important and always with all the children. I love to see the table covered with white linen, the *chalah* covered with an embroidered cover that my wife made. The silver *kiddush* cups for the wine. My silver cup, that was a present from my grandfather for my *britmilah*. The *shabbat* candles which my wife lights and also my daughters.

It was Friday afternoon, and as on every Friday I went for my nap. I had a dream ... It was the year 2000. It was a kibbutz. Socialism was the name of the game. They had red flags all over. You saw the fat women walking in the gardens, some carried laundry, some children. All were dressed in the same way, like a uniform: khaki short pants. You could see the big asses moving like balloons. Khaki shirts, 'tembel' hats. All were sunburned with red faces. Here and there they looked like a marching circus. A very serious one. Music was in the air, the International Socialist Hymn.

Then something terrible happened. Something was flying in the air. When it approached it was clear it was a *talis* (a prayer shawl: *talith* in Hebrew). That *talis* was flying in the air and it came down, right to the biggest and highest tower of the kibbutz.

Everybody was very excited; someone cried out: 'It is the devil.' A fat woman started screaming: 'It's the religious party with its propaganda.' Loudspeakers started to call everybody: 'To the conference room.' 'Fast, everybody to the conference room.' All were seated and waiting for the kibbutz secretary. He came, a very proud man, and said: 'We have an enemy flag on our highest tower. We cannot tolerate it. We have to resolve the problem now! Now!

They chose the best young men to get the *talis* down. One by one they climbed up, and tried very hard to get the *talis* down. But when they were almost at the top, somehow they could not get it. Somebody had the idea to try and shoot it with a bazooka or with a cannon, but the idea was not accepted. Somebody said that maybe it had to do with black magic, or maybe mystics. So they decided to ask the old man who knew about magic, religion and other mystics if he remembered something from the old days, the days that even people in a kibbutz knew about even though they had voted not to think about these terrible things any more. They were against socialism.

There was a man who knew about those things. He had a beard and did not speak very much. After a while he said that someone had to say *'Shemah Israel, adonai eloheinu adonai achad.'**

Members of the kibbutz started to scream, 'This is impossible! This cannot happen in our time. We are now in April 2000. This is not to be believed.' When they calmed down they decided that the old man should sacrifice himself for the kibbutz. He was the one who had to say it. They also decided that nobody was going to hear what he said and that everybody, I mean everybody, should be in their rooms. After an hour or so everything was organized and the old man stood in front of the tower with his head up to the talis and cried out: 'Shemah Israel, adonai eloheinu, adonai achad.' Nothing happened. The old man ran to his room and found a prayer book he had hidden years ago. He was not religious, he only kept it as a talisman. He ran again to the *talis* that waved with the wind. He cried out again, '*Shemah* . . .'. But nothing happened. He came back to the conference room and said, 'This is a sign from heaven or whatever you think it should be. We have to say "*Shemah*". All of us.'

---

* 'Hear, O Israel, the Lord is our God, the Lord is One.'

It took many hours to deliberate, and many more to decide how to say it. They finally decided. Everyone would say it. They decided that they would sing it all together with one melody. The hymn of the International Socialist Party.

Everyone was there, men, women, old, young, children. Then it happened: the *talis* fell very slowly, until it was on the shoulders of the old man from the kibbutz. At first they thought to tell him to leave the kibbutz, but after a while they decided that he was going to be the talisman, maybe the man with the prayer shawl . . .

I got up, my children called me for the *shabbat* . . . *kiddush*.

I Remember . . .

An old man walked barefoot at the seashore and looked at his footprints. Somehow he had the feeling that somebody walked next to him. He thought about God, and saw his life before his eyes, just like a motion picture. Every chapter was there, the happy and the sad.

'Oh God, when I needed you more than ever you left me alone. In my biggest problems I did not see your footprints next to mine in the sand . . . Why did you leave me? . . . Why did you do this to me?'

'The footprints you saw were not yours . . . They were mine . . . I had you in my arms . . .'

It was an early morning in Breslau, then Germany. It was already cold. The men from the SA and SS came to visit us. They asked for my father. I don't know if he was anyone special for them. He was just another Jew who had to be in a concentration camp. I was then two months old and I became the youngest hero of the family. It was the day after the *Kristallnacht*. My Aunt Edith knew that I was very hungry and I was just having my bottle. She took it away from me, and that's how the party began. I screamed so loud that even for the SS men it was impossible. They said 'Auf wiedersehen' and promised to return. Maybe they did; we were already in Berlin, at the Meinecke Strasse, for our papers to leave Germany. I was the youngest passenger on the *Columbus*, the last ship that left Germany with Jews. It was January 1939. I was only two and a half months old. My angel, the one that was sent to protect me, also left Germany. God left, too.

God left a sign: 'God does not live here anymore ...' Forty-eight years later, when I put my feet for the first time on German soil again, the sign was still there. God did not return. Funny, but this year *Chanukah* and Christmas are on the same date. Little children will sing beautiful songs. Festive songs. But who will listen? Maybe only the big and cold winds that carry six million Jewish souls and other innocent people who cannot understand what happened.

So, we had a new home: Bolivia. There was no country that wanted to give us shelter. Not even Bolivia. The new president did not want us, until his mother told him that she wanted to die in his palace if he did not let us in. Why? 'Because we are also Jews who were expelled from Spain a long time ago ...'

Bolivia is the most beautiful country in the world. When God created the world he gave each country its beauty, and when God finished he had a little bit of everything left and all of that he put into Bolivia. This country has everything – mountains, lakes, rivers, jungle, gold, silver, petrol, poverty, corruption; – but what is best about Bolivia is its music, which is like the singing wind. I told you before about the winds. This music is the melody of singing souls. People who suffered, and still do. Melodies of the soul. The Indian soul. The soul of mankind.

When I was about five years old and my sister Violeta two and a half years younger, we wanted to surprise our father for his birthday. He had a little aquarium with little fish. He loved them, and was very proud to have that little aquarium. Violeta and I had four coins together in our hands. We decided to buy something new for the aquarium. The coins we had were, for us, a fortune. We did not know what their value was.

I looked a bit funny in those days, with my short trousers and a sock always falling down. Violeta was a very proud young lady. Mr Goldstein was a very big man, about ten feet high.

'We would like to buy for our father these little two fishes.'

'Do you have any money?'

'Yes!' I said. 'We saved for a long time, it is our pocket money.' We showed our four coins very proudly: 'Is it enough?'

Mr Goldstein looked at the coins, and after a little while he said, 'Yes, it is enough.'

We walked home, very happy, with our bowl and the two little fish.

'Where did you steal those?' My father was a person of black and white. He did not understand; I did not understand. I only had very big tears in my eyes and was very offended. He took my little hand in his and went to Mr Goldstein's shop. I had to run all the way.

'Did my son buy these fishes here?'

'Yes, and he paid for them too.' Goldstein showed the four coins, our four coins. 'You see, my dear friend, what these coins can buy?'

Only then did my father understand what had really happened. It was for him the first time in his life that he saw colours. Not everything was black and white. He gave us a big kiss, and that was the last thing I remember. A few months later he left us and went to the United States. We never heard from him again. All the little fish died.

Many years later I was in the United States, in New York. I had a friend, Paul, who was a police officer. I loved to be in his patrol car and drive through New York's streets. One evening we heard on the radio that an accident had just happened and they needed blood. It was a rare type that they needed. I said to Paul, 'I have this type of blood. Let's go to the hospital.'

'Listen, young fellow, you are not a rich man, and you need a few dollars. Do you know you can make a few with your blood?'

'Blood is not for sale, it is a gift from God . . . please hurry.'

After I had donated, and the life of the young injured driver was safe, the doctor told me that the father of the young man wanted to thank me and give me some money. Then I saw Mr Goldstein again. The man with the fish shop, from La Paz, Bolivia. He did not recognize me because I was already a young man. But I recognized him. He was the same big man, only a bit greyer. He had not changed. I said to the doctor, 'It's nothing.' I went away. I did not want to destroy such a beautiful situation, just as Mr Goldstein did not when he saw the four coins in our little hands.

'Mountain and mountain never meet, men do, sometime, somewhere ...'

Grandfather, Grandmother

When my grandfather was a child, he was so beautiful that his parents had to make him ugly. They put his hair over his face, never dressed him nicely; they were afraid of 'the bad and evil eye', like Joseph in the Bible.

In the family they called him Ben Porat Joseph, because of his beauty, but his name was Louis. He learned the Torah, like any other young Jew, and later on he was in the wine business. The business of his father and grandfather.

It was a special wine, for the holydays, that was always ready for *Pesach*, and every time in new bottles, because it had to be kosher for *Pesach* (Passover). Since Jews were not allowed to have or possess land, there were lands that were rented from the *goyim*, and the vineyard was planted according to the Jewish law. The first three years you can not eat the grapes because they are *orlah*, like an uncircumcised boy. There were very strict laws, that the *goyim* learned and respected. Not because of their love for Jews, but because they got more money for the land. Also the *goyim* loved the 'Jewish' wine, for some reason it was better.

When my grandfather was eighteen, it was the time to get married, and in those times every Jewish religious family contacted a *shadchan*, a marriage-broker, if you can call him that.

Mr Gutfreund was a *shadchan*. He came with an offer; since everyone heard about my grandfather, they had already an eye on him. Mr Gutfreund found a beautiful girl, he said, who came from a very good family, 'Yiches', and was very talented. He also said that the young virgin lived in the United States, and that her father was very rich. Not only that, but he was willing to give one hundred thousand dollars . . .

My great-grandfather heard all what Gutfreund said, and smoking his pipe, said, 'No . . . This is no good. If she is beautiful, that is not a sin; that she comes from a good family could not be better. If she is talented, that is positive; that her father is rich, that can help. But one hundred thousand dollars! If they had asked this from us, it is understandable, with so many good sides, but that they offer it . . . something is wrong.'

'But I am almost eighteen . . .'

'Do not worry, my son, you are going to be married in three months.'

'But to whom?'

'In time, my son. In time.'

Three months later they were married. My grandmother was a very tiny woman, and my grandfather very tall. She had a secret beauty that was impossible to see with the eyes. She came from a very good family – the Nothmanns. I still remember when my grandparents celebrated sixty years together, sixty years married. They never had a fight, there was never a loud word. 'A *shiduch* from heaven,' Jews said.

Louis and Rosa were on the *Columbus** too. We were poor. When my father left, my mother remarried. My stepfather was a very cruel man. He hated my father, and I looked just like him. I think that my family invented the photocopy machine. Because we all look alike. My children, too. It is like a label on a bottle, you can't miss it. Every time I was in my grandparents' house, there were always the things I loved to eat. I don't know how my grandma did it. In such a tiny kitchen. We were poor. When the time for my *barmitzvah* came, I had to learn all the *parashah*, that part of the Torah that you read on *shabbat*, all of it.

A *barmitzvah* is very important, and generally every boy got a new suit. I did not. My grandparents found an old suit from Germany. They fixed it. They found an old shirt, where the collar had been put upside-down, but I looked as if I were the Prince of Wales. Anyhow, I felt I was.

* See page 11.

The day after my *barmitzvah*, my grandfather took me to a photographic studio and said to me, 'My son, you are thirteen now . . . you are a man. You have to work and make money.' The lady from the studio brought an apron and I put it on. She said to me, 'You see this floor. This is wood. You have to clean it very well, and then wash it with petrol; after that put wax on it and polish it until it looks like this mirror.'

I had big tears in my eyes, and I looked up to my grandfather for help: 'My son, if you do this well, you'll do everything in your life well.'

I worked very hard. The floor shone more brightly than the mirror. I don't know if it was the wax or my tears that made it shine. Every stage in my life I remembered my grandfather standing there, very proud.

I can still see my grandpa and grandmama in their little home in La Paz, Bolivia. I wish that they could see me now. I have a suit now, my own . . .

You Have to Know . . .

To be an antique dealer you have to have a few qualities: you have to be as patient as Job, as rich as Midas; to have the knowledge of Solomon, the years of Methuselah; and, lately, to be as crazy as Woody Allen.

Sheinkin Street. A quarter to two. Puchashevsky and I sat at the same table. He was having his tea and I my Turkish coffee. There was a rule, or a law, in that coffee house. The first dealer to come had the first choice, if a person came and offered to sell something. Then the second and the third, and so on.

Puchashevsky was the first. A woman approached with something wrapped in a newspaper. She started talking to me, and I made a sign to her to approach my partner at the table. She did. She unwrapped and displayed three glass cups. You could see that they were old, even nice. Puchashevsky asked the price and at the end he bought them for thirty lira. Other dealers came in and each one took a place, and started to order: coffee, tea, cake, cola . . . and so on. It was after two and it was a sunny day, so more tables were out than the usual three. Shashua asked Puchashevsky, when he saw the glass cups on the table, 'How much . . .' Puchashevsky looked at me first, because I was the second. I made a sign with my head, meaning go ahead.

'Look, I paid thirty and I want sixty.'

'Would you take fifty?'

'*Mazal* and *brachah*', that means good luck and blessing, a sign

38

that the deal was completed. Now the three glass cups were on Shashua's table. Isser was sitting next to Shashua. He started to look at the three pieces, once, twice and once more. 'Shashua, how much do you want for them?'

'You saw for how much I bought them – fifty. I want a hundred for them.'

Isser started to inspect again the objects, and after a few minutes he said, 'I offer you eighty.'

'You don't understand about antique glass, you have to know these objects, but if you give me ninety you can have them.'

'*Mazal* and *brachah!*' The glass objects moved to Isser's place. It was then twenty-five past two. Stieglitz passed. He did not sit. He just asked the price, but when Isser said 'Two hundred' Stieglitz walked away. Isser said to Shashua, 'He does not understand, he does not know.' Both laughed loudly. Berger was sitting at the end of the room. He came over to Isser.

'You don't know anything about antiques, although you think you do. I learned in Poland and then in France. I know, I'll give you a hundred and fifty for them.'

'If you offer me such a sum, you don't know what I have in my hands. If you knew, you would not offer so much.'

'So how much would you take, what is your very last price?'

'Because it is you, I'll give these to you for one hundred and eighty.'

'*Mazal* and *brachah.*'

The glass cups changed hands again, and tables.

Berger was asked again by some other dealer, later on, but he said that he bought them for himself, for his private collection. Two weeks later, when I passed his shop, I saw the cups in his shop window, on Dizengoff Street. After a month they were still there. A year after I saw them in the same place, only one thing changed: there was dust on them.

It was three years later that I was sitting at Berger's shop. An English dealer entered. He asked for the glass cups and Berger told him that the price was two hundred each. The English dealer asked, 'Two hundred what?' Berger immediately answered, 'Two hundred dollars, US dollars, for each. But I want to sell them together because I bought them together.'

The Englishman inspected the cups over and over again, but I noticed that he actually inspected one glass more carefully. He said, 'All right, I am going to buy them. Please wrap them up for me.' I saw that the man was impatient to leave.

When he left, I started to follow him. I had a feeling that something was going on. He entered a bookshop, and I saw that a young lady was taking out a book from the window. When the man left, I went in and asked for the same book. There it was: on the cover, the same glass. It dated from the time of Elizabeth I. I bought the book, to know – I had to know.

The glass cup was sold six months later at Sothebys, for eighteen thousand five hundred pounds.

You have to know . . .

The General

Each country in the world has a national hobby.

In the United States they have two: baseball and hot dogs. In England it is cricket. In Germany it is beer. South America has football. In Israel it is archaeology. It is a hobby, yes, but with several reasons. First, because it is what it is. Second, because every place in the country, wherever you make a hole you find antiquities. Wherever our neighbours make a hole, they find oil. Third, because it is to prove that we Jews lived here for thousands of years, and to find coins with Hebrew inscriptions that are over two thousand years old means something. It is a written proof. To find seals from the period of the Kings means that we are here at least three thousand years; and finally to find artifacts from the period of Abraham, four thousand.

In almost every house you see at least one archaeological object. This is because Israel is building up a new country and for two thousand years, since the destruction of the temple, nothing was done. Before we build anything new, we first excavate. The official excavations and the others.

In Rome, Roman artifacts are found; we have them, too. In Persia, Persian antiquities; we have them also. In Egypt, Egyptian scarabs; here we find them too. In Greece, Greek vases and coins; here, too. And so on ... Everybody was here, we still are.

To collect antiquities, the hobby, is like being addicted to drugs. The General was addicted, but not only that, he was

42

proud of it. Whatever he did, he did it so that everyone in the country knew.

We first met when I was wandering in the Upper Negev to see if anything was lying on the ground. He was looking for the same thing. He was a general and I was a young lieutenant. The General, I had heard before, had no friends. We became friends in one minute. We had something in our veins that was the same. The curiosity and the extreme need to have objects that can prove that we are the new Maccabees, looking for our heritage.

That was many years before I was an antique dealer. An authorized one. He was one already, but did not have a licence. He never did.

The General used to visit my shop, and then my gallery at least once a week. He used to come to my home, too. I was in his house, here and there. We always talked about the same subject, archaeology. To sell something to the General – I mean, to make some money – was almost impossible. In every transaction, if I did not get my money back, I lost. One day I had an idea: the General bought that day artifacts for one thousand lira, which was the actual price I paid for them. I asked the General for fifty cheques of twenty lira each. He sent one of his men to the bank and later on the fifty cheques arrived. He signed every one. Now everybody was happy. I used to sell the cheques for the same amount but in dollars, to tourists who were very happy that the famous General owed them money. The bank was happy that they did not have to pay the cheques. The General was happy that the cheques were not cashed, and he had the antiquities too. I was happy I made a profit: I still sell the General's cheques. They are famous now.

I don't know why I used to phone the General every time I had some new finds. I was also one of the very few who had his direct phone number. I think that the reason was the mutual interest and enthusiasm, and most of all, the excitement.

One day, I bought a wonderful collection of ancient pottery, from the period of the Kings, from Abou-Rommel, an antique dealer from the old city of Jerusalem. In normal times, it was very difficult to purchase something from this man. He played poker, and lost a very substantial sum of money. That was the time to buy, and make a nice profit.

The General was here, twenty minutes after my call. I used to

start counting the minutes from my call till he arrived. Sometimes he used to break his own record.

Here he was. He directly entered the little room, and saw the items on the table. He did not speak. After a while he said to me, 'I must have them, for my collection. How much do they cost?'

'I don't think they are for you. These are profit pieces, and I waited a long time for something like this.'

'That is not fair. Why did you call me?'

'Just to show them to you. Is it not enough?'

'No!'

All the time he was standing. Now he sat down, checking each piece again and again. 'You must sell them to me, I must have them in my collection. They complete a section of a whole period. Please let me have them.'

'Do you know how much I want for them?'

'We are friends for so many years, you should make only ten per cent on it.'

'Oh, really?'

'Look, do it for me this time. I'll do something for you next time.'

'OK, but only this time, if you promise that they go to your collection.'

'Of course.' He looked offended.

'OK, here is your bill.'

'I have no money now. Give me a little time and I'll bring it to you.'

'That I can't do. I just paid cash for it. No money and no antiquities?'

'Just a few days, that is all . . . please?'

'You win, General, a few days.'

Days passed, also weeks. No money. Two months later I was in New York. I have a friend there. An Armenian antique dealer. I went to visit him as usual. Then I saw that all the pottery vessels I had sold to the General were there. I told my friend the story and he told me that he purchased them from the General. He was as mad as I was. More, when he heard the price the General had not yet paid and the price he had got from the Armenian: five times more, in dollars! He gave me the artifacts, saying I should have them.

I phoned the General as soon as I got back, and told him that I had something very special for his collection. Twenty minutes later he was in my gallery. He went directly to my back room and saw the vessels on the table. He went white. 'Are they good for your collection? Do they complete a period of pottery vessels? Now listen very carefully, General, tomorrow at ten I want the money back for the Armenian in New York. Not one minute later.' He knew I meant business. The next morning the money was sent in an envelope.

The General lost one battle. My friendship.

The Treasure

The Yemenite Jews are without doubt the most exotic Jews. They lived in Yemen after the destruction of the first temple in 586 BC. The Yemenites represent an extraordinary group, which has survived under the most trying conditions.

Most of the Yemenite Jews came to Israel in the early fifties in an operation that was called 'the Magic Carpet'. The San'ani family came before. They came by foot at the beginning of the century. Some of them were ill. Many had to pay their passage through hostile people; with gold and jewellery. The San'ani family was a big one. The patriarch, Zechariah, was a venerable old man and the head of that big family. Fifty-two men, women and children. He died on his way to Jerusalem.

His wife Kadia was the leader now. It was very rare that a Jewish woman had that power, but she and her first-born had the gold and the jewellery.

The San'ani family was very religious, as almost all Jews in Yemen were. When they arrived in the Holy Land they settled in Rosh Ha-ayin, a place near the town of Petach-Tikvah. They lived in little houses, mostly built by themselves, with every material they could find.

In the early twenties life was very hard. The results of the Great War still affected the world. The San'ani family worked at everything they could. They were poor. Grandmother Kadia's was the address when there was an important occasion. She used to go,

47

when nobody saw her, to the field at night, and the next day she would go to the big city to sell what she had found.

Every wedding or *barmitzvah* or *britmilah* was always celebrated with a small party. These parties were always the most colourful ones and happy ones that one might dream of.

Everybody was worried about Grandmother Kadia, who was getting old. Here and there somebody in the family used to ask her about the gold and jewellery; and she chased everyone away: 'The gold is gone! It's in your stomach! Go to work, and study the Torah.' A few weeks later, Kadia died. Nobody knew where the treasure was, or if it existed. Everyone started digging here and there, but nothing was found. One year after Kadia died, parties were allowed. It is the Jewish law: no parties during the year of mourning. A little boy was born, and in eight days came the *britmilah* (circumcision ceremony) and there was no money. Everybody was sad in the San'ani family.

Shama was a young woman from the San'ani family. She was a widow. Her husband had been killed by robbers on his way to Israel. She lived alone with her five children. She was married when she was thirteen. At nineteen she was already a widow. Three days before the *britmilah*, she came to her cousin's house and put on the table the money needed for the party. That day everyone knew that she was the one who knew the secret.

After a while she was the most popular in the family, and every second day she had a marriage proposal.

I met Shama when she was over forty years old. She never remarried. That day she came in and offered a beautiful gold pendant. All handmade, and exotic. It was an antique and therefore it was worth much more than the gold it was made from: 'How much would you give me for this piece?'

'Three times its value in gold.'

'So much! Till now I only got the value of the gold, I mean, even less.'

'You did not know to whom to sell it.'

'I think you are honest. Next time if I sell something from Yemen I'll bring it to you.'

That was the beginning. Collectors used to come every time and ask about original Yemenite jewellery. Museums, too. The woman used to come now and then. She was always nicely dressed in her Yemenite outfit. For many years she used to come, and always telling me which party it was, and who was who in the San'ani family. One day Shama did not come; she had phoned before, but did not arrive.

Two months later I went to her home: 'She died.' All the family was there. Somebody asked me what I was doing there, and from where did I know Shama. I told them that she used to sell jewellery, and I told them that I even knew the names of the members of the family, who celebrated, and the nature of the party.

Shama asked to be buried in a nice dress, so she would look nice when she came to God. Like a bride. But they did not carry out her wish. Maybe they forgot, or they did not want to spend any money.

Several times members of the San'ani family used to come to my gallery and ask me if I knew where she hid the gold and jewellery. I did not know. I was told the story about the three tin boxes with gold that they brought from Yemen. One was robbed at the time Shama's husband was killed. The two others disappeared. They told me that they dug the field from north to south, east to west – and nothing. They even went to a *chacham*, a wise man, for consultation. He even wrote a *kamea*, an amulet. Nothing.

People used to say that everyone in the family suspected one another: Maybe he or she knew where the treasure was. Many years later a rabbi asked them if Shama left a wish. Somebody remembered. They even discussed it. The times were bad ones, and a dress like the one Shama wanted was very dear.

Shama's son, Baruch (the blessed), worked day and night, and four months later he ordered the dress. The dress his late mother had wanted. He opened the grave at night, which is forbidden and sinful. It was raining and cold. He was afraid of what he was doing. After so many years . . . He found the bones and put the dress in the tomb. He closed it again, and with his last tears and strength he put the stone back. It was three in the morning and very cold. He was dirty from the earth and sweat, and wanted to wash himself.

He did not want to wake his family, so he started to wash himself in the yard. The rain was stronger, and while the water was running he heard a metallic noise next to him. He bent down and saw part of a tin box. He started to excavate . . .

The treasure was there. Shama was probably nicely dressed when she met God.

Absurd True Stories

Stories were born in the country; there people have the time to tell and listen to them. Jokes were invented in the city, where people are in a rush. Absurd stories are the ones that are unbelievable, until they happen to you.

A Chinese antique dealer had a very tiny shop in Shanghai. On the floor was an authentic Ming Dynasty bowl. In that bowl was milk. Next to the bowl was a cat. It was lunch-time. An English dealer came into the shop, and when he saw the bowl he did not believe what his eyes saw. A real Ming Dynasty bowl. It was worth a fortune. To examine it better, he bent over and started to pet the cat.

'Oh, what a beautiful Siamese cat!'

'It is not Siamese. It is an ordinary simple cat.'

'Look at its colour. So beautiful, beige.'

'It is not beige. It is brown.'

'Yes ... if you say so. But he looks so young.'

'The cat is twelve years old.'

'I think I like your cat very much. Would you sell it to me?'

'How much would you pay. How much?'

'Because he is so nice, I'll give you twenty English pounds.'

'Twenty English pounds, for a cat that is not worth more than sixpence?'

'Absolutely!'

'How will you pay?'

'In cash.'

'I accept. Give me the money please.'

The English dealer took a twenty-pound note and gave it to the Chinese dealer. The Chinese handed the cat to the new owner. 'Thank you very much. I am very pleased. Now – excuse me – I would not like this poor cat to feel a stranger in my home. Please could you also give me the bowl, so he can have his milk in the same bowl he is used to?'

'I am very sorry, honourable sir, the bowl is not for sale. Because of this bowl, I have already sold two hundred cats.'

When a dealer is already well-known by others, strange things happen. It was in London. I went to an antiquities auction. To my surprise I made a mistake. I was a day too late, and the auction of that day was of Persian rugs. I didn't know anything about Persian carpets, I still don't. When I came to the auction there were two Persian dealers, from London, who recognized me. I waved hallo. I had the feeling that they were talking about me. When I approached, one came over and said to me, 'Here are two thousands pounds. Please go home.' I saw the transparent plastic envelope with the cash, and went home. Not home, but to my hotel.

A day later I found out what had happened. There was a carpet which they wanted to buy. They made a 'ring', which is that nobody from that group of dealers was going to bid a higher price. The carpet was going to go for the first-asked price. When they got the carpet, the dealers auctioned between themselves. That day the carpet was sold for ten times the price ... They thought that I had come for the same carpet.

The Scarab

It was after the Six Day War. I was in Jerusalem in the old city. Still in uniform. History records no other hallowed site, the uninterrupted veneration and faith of which is older than Jerusalem. The main gate of the old city was at that time the Damascus Gate, only some hundred metres from the Mandelbaum Gate. Mandelbaum was no gate at all; it was just a roadblock and its name came from the owners of the house that was half destroyed in the 1947 war.

Walking through the streets I saw an antique shop, and I had to go in. We spoke Arabic, but the man remembered some Hebrew. Among his items he had an ancient gold scarab, something that I never saw before. It was Egyptian and unique. I asked the price, and after a very long discussion I bought the scarab. It was very dear, even though I paid only thirty per cent of the price he asked. No Arab will ever give you something without an argument – he enjoys the argument more.

In my little shop in Beer Sheba I showed it first to a young lady who was visiting Israel for the first time. She fell in love with the scarab and held it so tight that the seal made its imprint on the palm of her hand. She said, very sure of herself, that the scarab would be hers, one day, when she had the money for it. She asked me not to sell it, and after a while repeated that somehow, some day, it would be hers. We laughed . . .

Months later, I sold the scarab to a lawyer from Canada, who wanted it for his wife's birthday. He was very happy with his choice, but his wife was not. A few months later, he came in with his wife, who had had an accident and who blamed the scarab for it. There was no problem in changing the scarab for another piece of antique jewellery, a gold pendant, and the deal was sealed. Everyone was happy. I was even happier, because I loved that scarab too.

I remembered what the Arab dealer told me: 'This was found near Tel ed-Duwier.' A few weeks later, I was in Tel-Aviv and went to see a friend of mine. He was a professor of archaeology, an Egyptologist, and was world-famous. He was very surprised when he first examined the scarab. Somehow it was too beautiful to be true. But in a while, after reading the hieroglyphics, there was no doubt. It was from the eighteenth dynasty. The base was incised. An S-shaped scroll on either side. Above and also below were two conventional gold signs. It was about 2,900 years old, parallel to the period of King David. It was the gold seal of Pharaoh Tuthmosis the Third.

Three months later I sold the scarab to a collector of seals in Germany. He was here in Israel, did not have the money, but said that he was going to do some business, and he'd send the cheque. A month later I received his letter saying how sorry he was, but he could not buy it.

I made a beautiful print of the scarab so, when displayed, the scarab's actual print could be seen, the same way the old king of Egypt did it. It was in the showcase and it was an attraction. I started to love the piece more and more, so I raised the price every time somebody asked. Somehow I did not want to sell it. Then came a very bad time in the country, and cash was hard to get.

For art and antique dealers it was even harder, because people buy art and antiques only in good times. In those times we had collectors. Today we have also investors. It was the Depression, so I started to sell some antiquities to dealers. The Arab dealer who sold me the scarab wanted to buy it back. At first I did not want to part with it, but I made him promise that in better times, if he didn't sell it, I would buy it back – with a profit, naturally.

Tourism in Israel was and is affected by terrorism. A little bomb can cancel a whole tourist season. We had many of those. We still have. Eventually times changed, and the sun was shining again.

I entered his shop hesitantly. Ten years had passed. As usual he offered me coffee, and we started talking about everything and nothing. I started to look at the things he had in his collection. I bought a few ancient coins. We had the usual arguments that were a feature of our dealings. I did not ask about the scarab. I was sure that he had already sold it. I did not want to hear it from him. I still had the scarab's print.

'You are not going to ask about the scarab? The gold one?'

'Tell me . . . did you sell it?'

'Three times . . . three times.'

'What happened?'

'The first time, I sold it to a collector. He was not happy with it, so I exchanged it for ancient coins. The second time it was sold by my son to someone who did not believe, after the purchase, that it was real gold, and he wanted to check it. I would not agree to damage the scarab to check the gold, so I gave him his money back. The third time, I sold it to a Persian dealer, who thought that everything bad that happened to him while he possessed the scarab was a curse. He is very superstitious. Maybe there is a curse, a pharaoh's curse.'

'I'll buy it back.'

'I'll sell it to you for the same price I paid you last time.'

'It's a deal.'

After so many years, the scarab returned to the same place it was before. The same showcase. I still had the stand and the print. I thought: look how things are. I was happy. It meant that I was to have the scarab, after so many years and so many hands.

Two years later, a beautiful woman was standing next to the showcase. I saw her in the mirror. I still was busy doing something. Then I was called: 'Excuse me, can you help me?'

'Yes?' Then I saw her. She was there. She had come for her scarab. Many years ago, she said that the gold scarab would be hers. Now it was.

13

The Ossuary

In describing Jewish tombs in old Israel, the Second Temple period is one of the richest. Little stone boxes are mentioned. These are called ossuaries. They exist in hundreds. A great number of them are perfectly plain, with no ornament or inscription. These ossuaries have no value for archaeologists or for dealers. Hundreds, however, have designs and inscriptions, some have both. Some even have artistic designs.

Inscriptions on the ossuaries supply an onomasticon for the Jews of the period. Most of the inscriptions are in what is called Hebrew-Aramaic. But Greek inscriptions too were common in that period. Inscriptions give the name of the man whose bones were in the box, and it is very rare for there to be additional details of identification.

Ossuaries were used for second burials. Most of them are found in Jerusalem and south of Jerusalem area, down to Hebron and south. But as usual there are exceptions.

Ossuaries vary in size, but are distinguished from sarcophagi in being much smaller. There are always some very rare cases, where the size may make the distinction difficult to make.

ANTIQUE DEALER ACCUSED
OF PROTECTING TOMB ROBBERS

This was a headline in the newspaper. Others had similar headlines. I was the antique dealer in the news. 'He was arrested and released on bail, till the trial.'

The detective from the police told the judge that the dealer did not report correctly to the authority, the Department of Antiquities, the possession of a unique sarcophagus he had, and falsely wrote in his inventory first, that the sarcophagus was actually a ossuary; second, that he bought the twelve ossuaries from Arab dealers who lived in Jerusalem. The Arab dealers denied that fact. The sarcophagus was worth six hundred thousand dollars. The police officer also said to the judge that the dealer did not have an explanation of the provenance of the ossuaries.

It was four o'clock in the morning when the phone rang: 'Who is this?'

'Hassan e'Keilan . . . Abu Yasser.' I recognized the voice which spoke Arabic.

'What is it, Abu Yasser, at this time of the night?'

'I have something very good for you . . . very good merchandise. Come to your shop, I am waiting.'

'Why not later, in the daytime. Let's say at seven or eight?'

'Come now, you never saw something like this.' (This is what Arab dealers always say, even if you have seen similar objects fifty times.)

'OK, give me twenty minutes.'

My wife was very angry, not only that I worked twelve hours a day, but now it was in the middle of the night

'I should have married a doctor, or a lawyer. At least they have normal hours.'

It was winter. Heavy winds blew, sixty miles an hour. It was raining and very cold. I said to myself that I must be crazy.

When I arrived, the truck was parked there. I recognized Abu Yasser, who was standing there with another six Arab merchants.

'Good morning, what have you brought this time?'

'Look . . . ' He pointed to the truck and I went over to see. There were twelve stone ossuaries. I held the flashlight and started to look all over. As far as I could see in the darkness, all the ossuaries were decorated with rosettes and other geometrical ornaments. Eleven were small, but one was big, very big. It was beautiful and unique. At first I thought it was a sarcophagus because it was about two metres long, but it had the same type of rosettes and ornaments that the ossuaries had. I was thrilled, and had to control my feelings. This was the time that the dealing would begin. If I started to ask the price now, I might never get them.

'I cannot see in the darkness . . . you will have to carry them all to the shop.'

'No, we talk here. We are not going to carry all of them to your shop and, if you don't buy them, to carry them back again to the truck.'

'Do you buy your antiques in the dark, when you can't see your hands before your eyes?'

Abu Yasser started to talk to his partners. There was a very big discussion. They understood that, if they brought the ossuaries to the gallery, it would affect the price. They knew it. I knew it. I had the advantage that it was night and dark. They continued to deliberate. Here and there, they tried to show me again the items with the flashlight, but I was firm, and it worked. They agreed.

It took a long time to carry, one by one, the ossuaries. Six men had to carry the big one. As they were on their way through the alley I saw its beauty. It was decorated with four beautiful rosettes on each side. Each one was different. On each extreme end there was a rosette too. I saw an inscription on one extreme end of the coffin, but I could not or did not want to identify it. It took over three hours, the negotiations. Sometimes they used to get up, to hold one of the small ossuaries and say it was over. No deal. Many times I told them to take the merchandise, and to sell it to somebody else. It was half past eight in the morning, and the deal was sealed.

Professor Ovadiah, from Tel-Aviv University, came to see me. He used to work for me, identifying some important antiquities, and then publishing them. That was good for both of us. He got the glory, and my antiquities were worth more after publication. When he saw the ossuary, he was absolutely sure that it was an ossuary and not a sarcophagus. That was also what I had written in my inventory, and now I was on trial because of fraudulent reporting to the authorities.

I had a very good lawyer – I needed one. I knew the real reason for the trial. The only way the government could get my big ossuary, without paying for it, was to find some offence and, since I was a licensed dealer, to revoke my licence, and therefore a legal reason to confiscate the ossuary.

Everybody told me that the judge was very severe. Even the police officer told me, 'You'll be in jail for five years.'

The most affected ones were my children. I told them that I was innocent, and actually I was very pleased that the judge was very severe because, I explained, if he is severe, he'll be severe both ways.

My wife and I worked very hard to find literature that could prove that very big ossuaries existed. And we actually found that the same man, who was behind the whole story, was writing a thesis about ... ossuaries. We found in his work that he mentioned one that was even bigger than mine.

It was the first time in my life that I was in court as a defendant. I was many times there as an expert witness.

The inspector from the antiquities department showed a very personal interest in my conviction, and this was very obvious. My lawyer made sure that the judge would notice it. I saw the judge's eyes, and there was no need for that.

When the government archaeologist testified, he mentioned the sizes of the ossuaries. I knew the man for over fifteen years. I also knew that he was an honest person, but now ... I was not so sure of anything. He told the court about sarcophagi and the similarity with mine. He also pointed out that an object like that should be in a museum, and not in private hands. When my lawyer asked if he was absolutely sure that it was a sarcophagus, showing the archaeological books we had, the answer was no. He was asked about the similarity with the known ossuaries, and the answer was yes.

It was the first time in history that an archaeological object was identified, as such, by a court.

I did not have to answer to charges. The case was closed as 'No Case to Answer'. I had no reason to ask Abu Yasser the reason he testified that he did not know me. I could only imagine that he knew the valuation that archaeologists had placed on my ossuary. I did not have to show the more than sixty cheques which I had paid, and which had been cashed by Abu Yasser.

'If that is the way the authorities handled this case, they did a very bad job. This court is sure that the property of the defendant was in danger and had to be protected by law ... '

I cried like a little boy. The court said there was not even one reason to bring the whole case to court. My children were happy. Dealers in Sheinkin Street did not whisper any more when they saw me. It was over: the dark clouds were gone. This time I waited for the morning's papers. I was news again: 'Antique Dealer Innocent!' 'Dealer [my name] Innocent!' 'Antique Dealer . . . No case.' Photographs of my ossuary were all over the papers. Until the trial I did not know that my ossuary was so . . . so valuable. I still have it. It is waiting for the right time and conditions to be in an Israeli museum. That is where it should be.

The Dowry Chest

America was discovered on 12 October 1492. That was the date when the first Jew made his first step in the new continent. Many families in South America have Jewish family names, though they do not know they come from Jewish ancestors.

In some of these Christian families, who are Roman Catholic and go to church every Sunday, strange things happen. They happen on Friday nights . . .

I was fifteen years old. I had a friend, who used to come to my home and I visited his. One Friday, in the evening, I saw his mother preparing two candles. She was very serious and set the candlesticks in a hidden corner. It was like a closet, and it seemed to be the place that the candles always were. She lit the candles, covered her eyes and prayed. The same way my mother lit the *shabbat* candles, and my grandmother as well. After she finished, she closed the doors of the closet, but not completely, for the air.

'Why do you light the candles?' I asked.

'I don't really know . . . but my mother used to, my grandmother did it, and my daughters will. It is like a family tradition.'

Their family name was Benavides. Ben Avi, a Hebrew name, meaning 'son of my father'.

A dowry chest is a wooden box in which the future bride brings her goods to her future husband. The very old ones had a special place for the bride's jewellery. Some of these dowry chests were decorated with the portraits of the young couple who were going to be married. Some had scenes from the history of the family they belong to, battles, or decorations from the king.

The dowry chest I was looking at, many years later, was beautiful. It was from the fifteenth century. It had a wonderful scene of a battle, that resembled a painting. An old one, a glorious one, showing how brave the man on the horse was. At the extreme ends below the iron handles there was a portrait of a man on one side, and a woman on the other. They were dressed in their best outfits. Inside it was covered with silk, and in the middle of the cover, from inside, was very fine and delicate needlework. It was a portrait of a very beautiful woman. The cover on the outside was decorated with the fleur-de-lis, the family symbol.

That dowry chest was there, in Boris's shop. He also had other pieces of antique furniture. The price was high and the man did not go down. Sometimes I used to buy from him fine antique Russian silver, but I would always notice the chest, standing there.

Boris was a Russian antique dealer. He really knew about antique silver. He worked once at the Hermitage Museum. He learned all that he knew by handling famous silver art objects. He was then one of the very few who knew Fabergé's work, and I learned from him, not because he was willing to teach, but because of his vanity to show that he knew more than me in that field. When I started to doubt, he showed me his books to prove it. That's how I learned more and more – and the dowry chest was still there.

Every time I used to ask him if he had a new price for the chest, and sometimes he used to go down just a few lira. We laughed. It was amusing.

I love antiques. But more I love the stories behind them. That a vase is three thousand years old and it came from the period of the Kings of Israel is important. For me it is important also where it was found, by whom, who had it last, and so on.

Boris and I were playing chess in my gallery. A man came in and offered an antique silver bowl. It was enamelled Russian silver. Boris did not move. I went to the other room to deal with the man. I bought the bowl. After the man left I showed it to Boris, who examined it very carefully with his magnifying glass.

'How much do you want for it?'

'Too much!'

'Now seriously, how much?'

'I propose a deal, no money involved. This beautiful silver bowl, for your ugly wooden chest.'

'I propose a deal, too. We exchange the pieces, but after the game. If you win, I add a hundred lira; and if I win, you do. It's a deal?'

'*Mazal* and *brachah*!'

I prepared some coffee and we continued the game. I was lucky. Boris made a mistake.

It was really a good day. I paid half for the bowl that Boris asked for the dowry chest. I even made some money. Boris was lucky, too; he sold the bowl for more than he asked for the chest.

When I took the dowry chest home, I started to check it. The wooden walls, from which the piece was built, were thick. My curiosity was great. I wanted to see what was under the embroidered silk. I also wanted to see what was behind the jewellery box inside the chest. I started to take it apart, one part from another. I put it upside down, when the cover was off – and there it was! You read in fairy tales about hidden treasures. Well, I found a little one. There was a special place made in the wood for five gold coins. Three were still there. On the other side there was a place with something in it. It looked like a letter or a document. Very slowly I took it out. It was the first time that the parchment saw light in four hundred years. It was a letter written in old Spanish to a certain man who was called David Benavides. It told the story how he was forced to convert to Christianity. The letter was signed 'Subieta', the Hebrew name for *Shivtah*, meaning from the tribe.

I wonder if this was from somebody in the family of a Christian woman who lit *shabbat* candles, in a corner, in a little closet, in a hidden corner of a room . . .

The Temple's Key

This story I heard from my grandfather. He heard it from his grandfather, and only God knows where it comes from, or how old it is. It comes for certain from a small town.

A little boy asked his mother, 'What is the truth?'

'The truth is like the most beautiful woman in the world. Long blonde hair, big black eyes, wonderful soft skin, lips like rubies, teeth like pearls ... and the most beautiful figure. That is the truth. Complete beauty!'

The question was never asked again. The years passed, and the young boy was now a young man. One day he stood in front of the door, with a little package. He was leaving. 'Goodbye mother, I must go.'

There was nothing she could say or do to stop her son: 'Where are you going?'

'To find the truth.'

The young man started to go from town to town, from village to village, in the near neighbourhood. Months passed. He crossed the frontier, and again travelled from town to town, from village to village. Years passed.

The young man was not young any more. One day, while he was resting in the woods, he saw something terrible: an old woman, crippled, stinking and dirty hair over her face. Her eyes were half closed and one of them jumping out. They were yellow-grey. Her arms and fingers were all convulsed. Her teeth were

brown, and her figure was bent forward. The man was terrified when he saw her.

'Who are you?'

'I am the truth.'

'That is impossible! My mama told me "The most beautiful woman in the world ... long blonde hair ... lips ... beautiful figure ... ' Now that I found you, what should I tell in my town?'

'Tell a lie.'

There were two antique dealers in Jerusalem, one shop next to the other. In the backyard they shared a water closet. Actually it was not a real one. It was a little room with a very deep hole in the ground. It was an old Arabic house. The door of this WC was a very old one and it had a very large iron key. Mussayef and Sweed were the antique dealers. They called their WC 'The Temple', and the key of that WC was called 'The Key of the Temple'.

There were always very big fights between these two men about whose turn it was to use it, and whose turn it was to clean it. There was only one key. Once it was in Mussayef's shop, and once it was in Sweed's. That's how you knew who was the last who visited the Temple.

Mussayef used to deal in archaeological objects and jewellery. Sweed used to specialize in everything. The big fights over the Temple and its key were sporadic – depending on how busy they were.

The big fight started when the key disappeared and the door was open. One of the children dropped the key into the hole.

'You have to pull it out!'

'No, I was the one who cleaned last.'

'It was your daughter who dropped it!'

'You did not see her. It was your son!'

The two men started to hit each other until the police came. At the police station, everybody laughed when they heard the name of the WC and its key.

Next morning, everybody could see the results of the fight. Mussayef had a black eye and Sweed had a plaster cast on his hand. The discussion about the Temple key question took hours. It was decided that, whoever was the one who could manage to bring the key out of the hole, he was the owner of the Temple. The loser was going to be paid out.

That very same day, Sweed started to fish out the key from the hole. He had a wooden stick with a line, with a fishing hook attached. No luck that day. The fish didn't bite. Next day was Mussayef's turn. He had a very large flagpole that he used for national holidays. He attached a big hook to it, and tried his luck. He pulled out the filthy key, holding it as a trophy, and called his neighbour:

'Come over here! Look what I got!' Sweed shrugged his shoulders. It was over. The Temple and its key were Mussayef's now, for good.

The big key used to hang on the right wall of Mussayef's shop. It was attached to an old copper chain.

A very famous actor stepped into Mussayef's shop. He looked all over and asked, pointing to the key, 'What's that?'

'The key to the Temple,' replied Mussayef, amused.

'Really?' he asked, very seriously.

'Really.' The dealer thought that the famous actor was joking.

'For how much would you sell it to me?'

'Five thousand dollars,' answered Mussayef, jokingly.

'It is from the temple?'

'It is from my Temple.'

'OK, I'll buy it.' Mussayef, who always told stories about crazy people, crazy tourists, well now he had crazy famous actors. He was making more money with that iron key than he paid for the complete 'Temple.'

Many years later I was in Chicago. I was visiting a Jewish institution which had a museum. A group of visitors was standing in front of an exhibit that I could not see. When the group left I approached the case. There was the key. The inscription read: 'The key to the Temple of Jerusalem'.

Triton

I had just had my coffee. The Jerusalem antique dealers had arrived. Every Monday they used to come to Tel-Aviv, to buy and sell. At two they were already with us, the Tel-Aviv dealers, at Sheinkin Street. I had just bought, from Garbash, a collection of Jewish ceremonial objects.

The Jerusalem table was very active in a discussion about a Roman sculpture. The dealers called me over to ask my opinion. 'Have you ever seen a dolphin's statue?'

'It is not a dolphin, it is a Roman fish.'

'It is not Roman, it is Greek, or maybe Hellenistic.'

'I don't think it is an antiquity at all.'

The men were discussing among themselves and did not give me a chance to answer. Jerusalem dealers know everything, even better than God. I looked at the photograph, and did not say anything.

'It could be a fake. Yes, even the British Museum, when they bought the head of Julius Caesar, thought it was Roman. It was not. It was a sculpture from the nineteenth century. I think this is modern.'

'The Arab dealer who sold it to me said it came from the sea.'

'Still, it is not a complete statue. You see, it is broken.'

I took a chair and sat next to them. It was a very interesting conversation. The piece was even more interesting, so I said, 'I would like to see it. Where is it?'

'In my car.'

We went over to the car. It was a beautiful piece, marble, and as far as I could identify its period it was Hellenistic – Roman. I asked about the price, and just standing there we came to an agreement. The dealer and I transported the sculpture to my car.

'What do you say, is it a fish or a dolphin?'

'Is it Roman?'

'Hellenistic?'

'I bought it.'

'That was a quick one.' Everybody burst into laughter.

'We'll see who did a quick one on who . . .'

'A Tel-Avivian can never do it to a Jerusalemite.'

It was four o'clock; we had to return to our shops, and the others to Jerusalem. 'Next time we'll bring sardines, in Tel-Aviv they buy everything.'

I was sitting in my gallery surrounded by books again. I had learned that the biggest capital a dealer could amass was his knowledge. This was gained by experience and books. I am rich in books. My grandfather used to say, 'The higher a person goes, the smaller he appears to people who cannot fly.' He was so right. You have to be on the same level.

After many hours, the closest I could get was that my dolphin was part of a bigger sculpture, not from a complete dolphin, but from a statue of the mythical world.

Triton was the son of Poseidon and Amphitrite. In mythology he is described as living with them, in the golden palace in the depths of the sea. The mythical Lake Tritonis, near the Mediterranean Sea. The Libyan coast.

Triton was represented as a man in his upper parts and terminating in a dolphin's tail.

My part of the sculpture was found in the sea. It had seashells encrusted, so it was probably on a ship that sank. If it was from a ship, then the upper part was found or is going to be found.

I had the piece for many years, and it was probably the only item that people never asked about. I did not care, because it became part of the decoration of the gallery.

Years later, while I was going through old sales catalogues, I saw a statue of Triton, though the description was Centauro-Triton; but what caught my eye was the seashells on the sculpture in the catalogue. Could it be?

My next trip to New York was to find out the whereabouts of

that sculpture. I had to know. The piece was sold to a collector, who later on sold it to a Californian dealer.

Antique dealers have good memories, so when I called, the man remembered. It was not far away. It was in California in a private museum. It was not difficult to receive photographs of the piece, but what was more important than everything was the part that was broken in the statue.

Home again with this new material, I made a design, drawing the outline of the broken piece, and the outline of the part that was broken on my sculpture. They fitted. Now I was sure.

'If Muhammad does not come to the mountain, the mountain comes to Muhammad'. An old Arabic proverb. I now had to sell my dolphin to its torso, so now, after more than two thousand years, they could be together again.

I wrote a letter offering a big sum for Triton's torso. I explained that I had the dolphin tail, and it would be a shame for those two pieces not to be one again. I included the photograph, and of course the drawings I made to compare the broken parts, that now fitted together. The reply came very soon, as I had expected: a similar offer for the piece I had. I said to myself, '*Mazal ve-beracha*.'

Those Tel-Aviv antique dealers buy everything, even sardines . . .

A Page from a *Machzor**

A Hebrew illuminated manuscript is a collector's dream. It is the dream of every museum which exhibits Jewish ceremonial art. It is a dream to the dealer who can offer one for sale. Just to hold one once is an experience that is difficult to explain. It is like holding a very important antique piece of art which combines with history, mystery and enormous value.

It is impossible to say for certain how far back the history of Hebrew illuminated manuscripts goes. Medieval religious folk-lore created figurine decorations on these illuminated pieces of art and, even being so rare, their naive art is actually their beauty. The period of Islam is the earliest period from which we can date manuscripts, the Hebrew and the Christian. All deal with sacred biblical texts and the marginal decoration or the opening letters were embossed in gold.

If such an object of art appears on the market, it is offered only to big dealers. Large sums of money are involved. Once, I was offered one.

*   *   *

Dealers in the coffee house in Sheinkin Street were talking about the rumours they had heard of a manuscript, a Hebrew one, for sale in Europe. Nobody knew exactly which country it was. For

* A prayer book for festivals.

weeks the rumour spread, and every time there was another detail, but, if all the facts were put together, nothing was really clear.

A Persian dealer phoned one day and said that in Vienna there was a parchment in Hebrew for sale. He said that it had been taken out from behind the Iron Curtain. He could not say the place. I was asked to go to Vienna and see the man who had it for sale, but not before I promised a commission to the Persian dealer, if I was the one who was going to buy it.

I arrived in Vienna in the morning, hoping to be back in Tel-Aviv in the evening. So the first thing I did was to phone Hans, the man with the manuscript. He said that I could see him in the evening. When I asked him to meet me in the hotel, he answered that it would be much nicer to be in a place with a drink and some music. That was not exactly the way I was used to doing business. But in Rome you have to do what the Romans do; and in Vienna. OK, I agreed.

I passed that day looking at the shops, and thinking about what the parchment would look like. I had in my memory the illuminated manuscripts that I had seen in museums and those that were in private hands. There were not many. I even started to think who might be the collector or museum to sell it to.

It was eight o'clock at last. I took a taxi and found the pub with no difficulty. I entered. A man approached. He asked my name. I told him, and asked if he were Hans. The man said yes, and we went to sit at his table. There were two empty beer glasses on one side of the table. That meant that he had been waiting for me for some time.

'What will you have?'

'A small beer.'

'You see, I am a little afraid that somebody can see me. I am a smuggler of art from the East. I have to be very careful.'

'I understand, but here it is a little bit dark to see.'

'No, it is all right here.' He took out from a plastic bag something that was framed with glass. It was then I saw it. It was a page from a *machzor*. A prayerbook for the holy days. It was a page that was decorated with big Hebrew letters in gold. I wanted to open the frame to examine it better, but he did not allow it. He said, 'It is not mine. You can not do anything to it. I am responsible for it.'

I got up and went to a place that had better light. I saw the cracks in the parchment. I started to look again with my magnifying glass. It looked OK. Somehow I had the feeling I had seen something very similar. I bought the piece. I still could catch a late plane home. I did.

It was four o'clock in the morning when my wife and I started to look up in the books of Judaica and illuminated manuscripts. When we finished the books, we were sure that the illumination was from the fifteenth century. I also told my wife that it had to be from Germany. I told her that I remembered seeing something like it somewhere.

It was eight o'clock in the morning. We had more cigarettes and coffee. I said that I was going to the gallery to bring some more books. We were very excited. An hour later I was back. We started all over again. Books and more books. Cigarettes, and more coffee.

Suddenly I jumped up as if something inside me had exploded. I ran to the bedroom and took down the calendar that was hanging on the wall. It was the calendar with Jewish ceremonial art prints. Objects that were in the museum. I started looking through the pages and I found the same manuscript. I put it on the table and showed it to my wife.

'Maybe what you bought is stolen from the museum?'

'I don't think so.' I started to open the frame. After I had the glass off I saw that what I had bought was in fact another page from the same calendar.

'I have been taken . . . It is the same paper. It is a print on which they put some oil, some cracks . . . to make it look old. Now I understand the reason for meeting me in the pub. It was a trap. I think that the Persian knew it as well. All this was well planned. The rumours first and then the call.'

A few hours later I was in the Persian's shop. He saw my face and understood. I blamed him for all, and held him responsible. I knew that he had not the money to give me back. I started to make an inventory of his shop. I selected a collection of Judaica objects at selling price – not dealer's price. I ordered him to give me a box for them. He started to argue. I offered him an alternative – the police. He brought the box.

The Cursed Iron Gate

In the Judean mountains are caves. These caves were the shelter of the people who escaped from danger. David was one of them. Later he was the king of Israel.

About nine hundred years later people escaped to the caves when the city was destroyed. Jerusalem. Among the most famous are the Dead Sea caves. People trying to save their lives took with them little things they could carry, religious and personal utensils. They locked their doors when they fled, looking once more to the burning city, and took the keys with them. Yes, there existed keys two thousand years ago. They did not return. Yigael Yadin found those keys in the caves. They do not open doors any more. They open history.

Yom Kippur is the holiest day of the year. One of the outstanding features of Yom Kippur is the confession of sins, since without confession there cannot be repentance. Its origin is in the confession recited by the high priest on the Day of Atonement.

Kol Nidre is the evening service of Yom Kippur which precedes the Day of Atonement. It is in Aramaic. The worshippers proclaim that all their personal vows, oaths and promises that they made unwittingly or rashly or did not know about, that cannot be fulfilled during the year, should be considered null and void. They do not exist any more. The origins of Kol Nidre are unknown. I think Kol Nidre was born with the expulsion of Jews from Spain. Many Jews at that period promised to be Christians and accept the new faith.

Kol Nidre was for them. It still is.

*   *   *

In Zagreb, the place where they lived, the old grandmother used to tell stories about the family. The old grandmother was once married to a Gentile. He died many years before. Her daughter was married to a Gentile who left Zagreb with another woman. Little Anita loved to hear her grandmother's stories. She always used to tell them when Yom Kippur knocked at the door. Every year the same stories.

That year it was different. It was a new story about a forgotten uncle who left Zagreb when the grandmother was very young. He lived in Paris now, if he still was alive.

Uncle Abraham was the only one who knew the secrets of the family. He was old enough to understand them, when he heard them. Uncle Abraham was also the only living person from the family who had the relics that had survived from the past. Grandmother said that they came from Spain many years ago, and that was the family's origin.

Toledo was the place where for centuries Jews lived. Many think that it was from the period after the destruction of the temple, in the year 70 CE. Famous personalities from the Jewish world lived there. Hebrew books were written, Jewish life flourished. It was the fifteenth century.

Jews were expelled from Spain and emigrated to other countries. Europe and the New World.

Anita and her mother came to Bolivia after the war. Members of that family were killed by the Nazis. Some of them had only a few drops of Jewish blood in their veins. For the Nazis it did not matter – one drop of Jewish blood was enough.

Anita and I were very young. I loved to hear the stories she heard from her grandmother. She loved to hear the ones that I heard.

'You should go to your uncle in Paris before it is too late.'

'Maybe he is not alive any more.'

'You must find out, I think it is important.'

'I'll ask my mother to write.'

For us, these stories meant an identity. I was born in Germany. Was I a German?

I was three months old when I came to Bolivia. Was I a Bolivian? It was the same for Anita. She came from Zagreb. Was she Yugoslavian? It was very important for us to have an identity.

Weeks later, Anita was very happy. She received an invitation from her uncle. He was over ninety years old, and wanted to see her.

A month later Anita was back. Not only did she have a wonderful time in Paris, but she was richer now – her uncle had given her all that he had.

'He was a very strange man. At the beginning he did not trust me. It took over a week until he started to tell me about the family. He had a little wooden box where he hid his money. There were also a few letters that were very old. Some of them were from his great-grandfather. They were written in Hebrew. He could not read them. In the box he had also a big iron key. He told me that the key belonged to the house that the family lived in, in Toledo. When they left Spain they kept the key. They hoped to return some day, when the sea was calm again. The key passed family hands from one generation to another. Now I have it.'

'Isn't it fantastic! One day you are going to be in Spain, with your key in your hand, and open a door that was closed for over four hundred years?'

'If that day comes, I want you next to me.'

'I'll be there, with you.'

A few months later I parted from Anita. I came to Israel. Later on I heard that Anita had moved to America. I did not hear from her or her whereabouts from anybody else. I received the notice that her mother had died, and I was very sorry. Somehow I had the need to contact her during the years, and in that very special moment of pain and sorrow.

A few years ago I was in Spain. I had to go to Toledo, not only because of the Jewish history that the city had, but also because of Anita. I still had her in my memory and in my heart.

In a little bar I heard stories about legends of the people in the city. I loved them. My thirst for more brought me to a man who knew more stories. He was the man with the guitar. He was a gipsy. A real one. He really was. He was wearing a few shirts that could be seen under his two coats under an old raincoat. He invited me to his home for lunch and a glass of wine. It was a little one-room house. A tired, thin dog was supposed to guard the nothing that the man owned. He was poor. He brought out an old wooden tray where he started to cut very old bread with his pocket knife. He smashed it with a few tomatoes, and then added some oil. He then went through this with his bare hands. I had to look away at something else; even so, I could just see what he was doing.

At first I did not want to eat. I tried to excuse myself, but he insisted. So I started to eat. The man brought out two dirty glasses and washed them in a big bowl. The wine spurted out of the big bottle.

'There is an old house where the Jews lived. I'll take you there tomorrow. That old house is cursed. There are many stories that people tell of what happened, many years ago. It was the period of Isabel La Catolica. The Inquisition – God forgive us! It was called the Holy Office Court that was appointed by the Church, to suppress heresy. That was for about one hundred years.

'Jews, Arabs and gipsies were killed if they did not convert to Christianity. They were taken to the plaza and burnt to ashes.

'This cursed house had a fence made of solid iron, with a big iron door. People tried many times to open that door; but somehow there were always people who were against it. They were afraid of the spirits. God forgive!

'That door was once the back entrance to the house, by the side of which a narrow alley passed. It was so narrow that a carriage pulled by horses had almost no space, and when it passed people used to jump away into that house.

'Every year, ever since, the Holy Virgin is the one who has to bless that place.

'One day a woman came to Toledo. She was a tourist from America. She was with her husband and her children. She had a paper in her hand. It was as though she was guided by a map. People were very friendly to her until she came to the cursed house. People knew the story. She was sure that was the house she was looking for. She took out of her purse a big iron key. She went and tried every old door. Many of those doors had new locks, but the old ones were still there. Many people came over to see what was happening. The woman continued to try every door. People asked her to try the fence, the big iron gate. God bless us! She did. She put the key in and started to turn. At first it was very hard, and someone ran to bring some oil. She tried again, and it started to turn, making a yelling noise. A cry of pain. And it was open! People knelt and started praying . . . ' The curse had ended.

I did not need any further explanation. I knew, in my heart, that Anita had returned.

A Museum Piece

Garbash and I used to meet early at Nahum's place. It was an early morning coffee shop. It was also good for a late vodka, for those who found the night too short.

Nahum had the best coffee in Tel-Aviv, and Shoshana, his wife, made the best sandwiches. He used to call people, 'Hey, you idiot!' – even people he never saw before in his life. Sometimes when somebody was angry at him he corrected himself: 'Excuse me, Mister Idiot.' Then he would glance at us and say: 'You see, I am polite, I said Mister.'

Almost every day it was either me who paid for the coffee or it was Vladek. (Garbash was what most people called him, to us he was Vladek.)

Vladek met people in the morning, there at Nahum's place, as if it was his office. When somebody approached, he took the man for a little walk. Later on I found out that he helped all kinds of people who were in financial trouble. Most of them were people from Poland. Vladek was a short man, strongly built. The biggest thing he had in his body was his heart; there was very little room left for the bones, etc.

We were a small group of antique dealers who met in the early morning. Puchashevsky had his early tea. Stieglitz used to sit only to have a glass of milk, when one of us explicitly announced that we were going to pay for it. Sometimes a miracle happened and Stieglitz invited one of us for a cup of coffee. He had a system: he always was looking for change in his pockets that he knew well he did not have.

There were good times for Vladek, and there were others. The others were when he remembered that his family was killed before his eyes by the Nazis. There were the times Vladek started his day with a schnaps, or with a submarine – his name for a whisky in beer.

During the war he was with the partisans in the woods. He had many stories. Stories of war.

Leo Grawosky was a partisan. He was called by his fellow men 'the Aristocrat'. Even in the woods with all the war troubles and battles he had with him a pillow, and something that looked like a little wooden chair or stand. Actually it was an old bookstand that he used to sit on.

The pillow was a very hard one and he used it only at night under his head. He never let anybody touch it, and he never sat on it. He used to tell his friends that he had a photo album inside. When they walked through the woods he carried that pillow on his shoulder.

Each of those Jewish partisans had seen horrors, most of them had lost their dearest ones. Leo Grawosky was alone in this world. Not one of his family was alive.

Leo Grawosky came from a very noble family; the Grawoskys were considered high society in Poland and in Germany. The German part was not religious and was more assimilated. There were intermarriages, something that was inconceivable in the Polish side of the family.

Leo Grawosky prayed every day. He had a little *siddur*, a prayerbook, and from his *talith* he made his undershirt. He had also a Jewish calendar and was the one who reminded everyone in the group that a new holyday was coming, or if it was *Shabbat Rosh Chodesh* (the first *shabbat*, when the new month is blessed). At the beginning people did not want to know about Jewish festivities; it was not the time for it. It was war. Others were angry at Grawosky with his religious customs: 'If the God of Israel exists, why does he permit those killings, why?'

Grawosky answered, 'I am not God's ambassador. If God takes care of a worm under a stone, God will take care of us. I am sure of it!'

One night, Leo Grawosky fell from a little hill. He had a broken leg. Partisans had to leave him behind in a little village. They had to continue. That night the Nazis killed most of them; only two survived and luckily found shelter in another village.

In the early sixties, Grawosky lived in Belgium. He did not work any more. He never remarried and never forgot. Not his dearest ones. Not the war.

It was a summer when he first came to Israel. Leo Grawosky entered the gallery announcing, almost solemnly, that he was not able to buy anything. He just wanted to see antique Judaica objects. He was interested only in the old Polish ones. Some things he saw reminded him of home. Leo Grawosky was a person you could talk to for hours.

'I have something very important. It is actually the only thing I possess from home. From the old country.'

'What is it?'

'It's a Bible. It is heavy, and you would not believe it, but I had this Bible with me during the whole war.'

'Is it very old?'

'Oh, yes. It is from the seventeenth century. It belonged to my family. Many of the names, I mean members of my family, are written inside the cover.'

'I would love to see it.'

'I'll bring it in tomorrow. You know, I even have its original wooden stand.'

The next morning Leo Grawosky came with his Bible. It was a museum piece. A big book bound in red-brown leather, with a superb silver frame. It was thrilling to go through the pages. It was so well preserved that it was difficult to believe that this Bible had been in Leo Grawosky's pillow, and survived. All those years in the woods with the partisans.

'I want to donate it to an institution or a museum, in memory of my family. My wife, my children, my parents.'

'I think you should do it. It is wonderful.'

'I even saved some money, you know, for the dedication plate. I want it in silver. We Grawoskys loved silver, and we had a big collection of silverware.'

I saw the poor gentleman of today in the glorious times of the past. A little silver plaque for a museum-piece Bible.

Six years later I saw him again. He was carrying the Bible on his shoulder, maybe the same way he did many years ago in the woods. Under his arm was the wooden stand.

'What happened?' I asked, surprised, when I saw him.

'Don't ask!' – A typically Jewish answer, when somebody wants to tell his story. 'I went to an institution and saw the director. They had a little museum, which I thought was the right place for my Bible to be. I told him that it was a museum piece. He agreed. It was a museum piece. I asked him only to build for my Bible a little showcase. I handed him the little silver plaque I ordered to be attached to it. The man agreed. He told me that the next time I came for a visit, everything would be ready.' The old man lit another cigarette; it was his third. He continued:

'I saved a whole year for the ticket, and went to see the director again. I had to. When I was in the exhibit room I did not see my Bible. He explained that they could not build the case, but promised that the next time I came it would be ready.' Leo Grawosky lit another cigarette. He held it between his two fingers that were yellow-brown, the trace of thousands of cigarettes.

'A year later or so, I returned. I was sure that this time everything was in order. It wasn't. No showcase. No Bible. I was furious and demanded an explanation. Again the director tried very hard to calm me down. He said next year it would be on display. They had many problems in the institution. I said that the next time if I don't see my Bible displayed I'll take it back. A year later I could not return. I was ill. In the old-people's home, I counted the days to be better and return, maybe for the last time, to see my Bible displayed, and close my eyes for ever.'

I brought a cup of tea and offered it to him.

'Please, more sugar, dear friend. I need a lot of sugar to sweeten this bitterness. Two years later I went to this museum and bought a ticket. Like anybody else. I started to look around hoping to find my Bible. It was not there. I rushed to the director and he did not know what to say. I demanded my Bible back immediately. He started to look in the drawer and did not find the book. He called people who worked there, but nobody knew. They started to look all over, and after two hours somebody came with my Bible in his hands. It was all dirty and dusty. Eventually they found the wooden stand as well. I want now to sell this Bible and donate the money to charity.'

'This is a museum piece. People should see it.'

'I am too old now. You do whatever you think is right.'

'I'll do what I can.'

'My shoulders are too weak to carry it again. Please let me know whatever you do with it. But promise it should go into good hands. By the way, here . . . here, take this. I think I don't need this any more.' Leo Grawosky handed over the little silver dedication plaque: 'In memory of . . . '

I sold the Bible to another very big institution. The price was very high. In the conditions of sale it was stipulated that a special case was to be built. The Bible was to be displayed open at the chapter of the Exodus. A little plaque was to go inside the case. The one that Leo Grawosky put in my hands. The cheque should be sent to Grawosky directly.

In the newspaper was the institution's press release: 'A very rare Bible has been purchased. A museum piece.'

Nahum is dead now. Vladek is dead. Leo Grawosky is also dead. They were museum pieces. Monuments to mankind.

Sheinkin Street

The best days to hear antique dealers' stories are the rainy ones. The rainy days are also the best to sell antiques to collectors. Somehow those are the days when collectors have to warm themselves with a new item for their collections.

The best place to listen to those stories was at the Sheinkin Street coffee shop, as usual, between two and four in the afternoon.

It was January in Tel-Aviv. People said that it was the worst winter we ever had in the Holy Land. They say the same thing every year.

Two tables were pushed together to make a big one. Behind us was the bar. I don't know why, but that day was a special one. Maybe because we had a bottle of white wine on the table and the dealers were in the mood to tell stories.

'Anyone who ever visited the Cairo Museum with an Egyptian guide will believe that this story is a real one.'

'OK, tell us.'

The man held the bottle and filled his glass. 'One morning, early, an American tourist visited an antique shop in Cairo. He was greeted by the owner: "I have something very special to show you, a very special price."

'"What is it?"

'"It is in the back room. Come in," said the man with a special mysterious look. They entered the room and there was a shelf with cardboard boxes. He went and took one, and opened it. It was a skull. A human skull.

'"What is this?"

'"This is the skull of Cleopatra. The famous queen."

'"Really?"

'"Really."

'At that moment, in came another American tourist, who was attended to by the dealer's son.

'"I have something very special to show you. I will give you a very special price."

'They entered the back room, where his father was with the other tourist, went to the shelf and took another box. He opened it and inside was a small skull.

'"What is this?" asked Tourist Number Two.

'"This is the skull of Cleopatra, the famous queen."

'"How come? This is impossible," said Tourist Number One.

'The old dealer looked at him, very seriously: "This little one is when she was young, and this one . . ."

'My story is even better. Listen to this one: Once I was in the flea market in Jaffa. I was just looking around when I saw two men who caught my attention. One was holding one shoe and was offering it to a man who had two legs. Yes, I tell you, only one shoe. They were discussing the price. At the end I saw the man paying, and the seller handed him that one shoe. That day was my biggest lesson in antique dealing. I learned that everything can be sold, even one single shoe. By the way, I think that it was not even the right size.'

'Maybe it was a museum piece.'

'What is a museum piece?'

'A museum piece is something that you see in a shop and don't believe that it is real, until you see it in the museum.'

'A piece you see in a museum is a fake, but you believe it is real because it is there.'

'It is like the Julius Caesar head, that the British Museum bought, believing it was Roman, and it was made in the nine-teenth century. The funny thing is that now that they know, they will never admit it. They will tell you: "This piece is still being investigated."'

Another bottle of wine was ordered.

'In the Metropolitan they have the famous Etruscan Warrior. It was referred to in many books as a "masterpiece", until they found the man who still makes them. In Greece. This poor artisan never tried to take anything. He just made these beautiful sculptures.'

'A museum piece is something not important you sell to the museum. It becomes important the minute that the museum buys it.'

'A museum piece is one which was stolen from a museum.'

'A museum piece is one you pay money to see and cannot touch; while in a shop you can touch it without paying.'

'Once a very beautiful young woman came into my gallery. She was American, very rich, sophisticated, and did not know what to do with herself.'

'I wish she had come into my shop!'

'She started looking all over. Nothing really interested her. She looked at her arm and said: "I need a bracelet, do you have one?"

'I went to the showcase where I had a very beautiful antique bracelet. She put it on and you could see that she loved it.

'"What is it?"

'"It is an original, eighteenth-century Bedouin bracelet. It is solid, very fine silver. Here, you see, these are the silver marks. I can show them to you in the silver marks book."

'"No, it's not necessary. I believe you. But . . . it is not enough."

'"What do you mean by that?"

'"I need a story."

'"Well, I tell you again. This is an original bracelet from the eighteenth . . ."

'She interrupted: "Yes, I understand, but still I need a story. Without a story I cannot buy it."

'Now I understood. I asked her to sit down and said, "This bracelet was on the arm of a Bedouin prince. He had a very beautiful Arabian white horse. One day he saw a beautiful Bedouin girl. He said, 'You are mine.' He carried her to his horse, and put this bracelet on her arm . . ."

'"I'll buy it. This is wonderful. Why didn't you tell me before. How much is this bracelet?"

'What time is it?'
'Four o'clock.'
'Time to go.'

We took our raincoats and walked into the rainy street. We had to rush to open our shops – maybe a collector was already waiting for something to add to his collection – and feel warmer.

El Tapado

When I was about nine years old we used to live next door to a famous archaeologist. He came from Germany also. He was the one who was going to bring civilization a birthday present. A new chapter of the Incas.

He excavated in Tihuanacu and other places. He brought home hundreds of cardboard boxes with ancient pottery.

He had two sons who were not interested in what he was doing. I was. I used to sit there for hours watching him examine and catalogue the different items. He talked to himself and I thought he was talking to me.

There were so many finds – especially the broken ones that he wanted me to throw away. I did not. I used to take them to the cellar of our house. They were my treasures. I did not have many toys to play with. Nobody bought me puzzle games that I loved so much. I saw them in other children's houses, on their birthdays, when I was invited.

The cellar of our house was also my hiding place. That was the place where I used to talk to my father, who was gone, in my imagination. That was also the place where I complained to my father about the very bad treatment I received from my stepfather.

All these things happened while I was trying to put together the broken pieces of pottery I was supposed to have thrown away. Today we call it 'restoring archaeology'. The whole thing was so fascinating that I even succeeded in reconstructing a few complete pieces. I displayed them on tin cans in the cellar. Once the professor and I were sitting in his office. He showed me a small jug that he found. It was decorated with paintings. 'You see, my son, here was a handle that is missing.' I said no, it was not a handle, but a little puma's head. He looked at me very surprised. I had to confess that I had glued together a similar piece. I told the whole story very fast. I usually did, when I did something wrong. I didn't throw away the broken pieces, for which I got paid a few coins.

Moments later, the professor visited my museum. I still see him entering, through the little window, to see my exhibition. He smiled at me very proudly.

At the age of fifteen we had a teacher we loved very much. He taught us history and Spanish. I was very good at those two subjects.

One day, he received an offer to teach in another country. We could not bear to separate. We were standing at the railroad station and talking to our teacher who was in the train looking through the window. He gave us instructions, and told us to be nice to his substitute. My two best friends and I had other ideas.

The train started to blow its whistle, and my teacher and his family started to wave goodbye. Everybody saw the train moving. The carriage where my teacher was did not move. My friends and I smiled with malice. The train was gone. My teacher stayed.

Jaime was a very dear friend of mine. His family owned a very old house from the colonial period. The house was in the city of Potosi.

Potosi had a very rich mountain, all silver. In Potosi is also *La Casa de la Moneda*. A very famous house where the Spanish coins were minted. It is said that there was so much silver that a bridge of pure silver could be built between Bolivia and Spain.

The Spaniards needed manpower, and they used the poor Indians who died in the *socabon*, the mines. They tried bringing in slaves from Africa for that painful work. Those slaves lived in the upper part in *La Casa de la Moneda*, where they were chained at night. The slaves used to steal a few silver pieces and made holes in the walls to hide them. These holes were called *tapados*, the covered ones.

The legends about the *tapados* are told in every house in Sucre and Potosi, the places where the Spaniards lived. Most of these very old houses have very thick walls.

The slaves of Africa did not survive. It was too cold for them, they could not get used to the height, and they could not breathe in the mines.

Jaime invited me for a few days with his family in Potosi. It was the first time in my life that I had a holiday. It was only for a few days.

When we were on the train the stories of the *tapados* were in the air, and even more in our dreams we longed to find one. Legend also had it that some people were very rich now. They had found a *tapado*.

The most thrilling of the *tapado* legends is how to find them. It is said that in the middle of the night you see fire on the wall. A little flame that comes out of the wall. That is the place where the hidden *tapado* is. You are supposed, when you see it, to go to the place immediately, and start digging.

Jaime and I were given a room downstairs. It was one of the rooms that was once for the servants of the house.

When Jaime and I entered that room, we were still talking about the *tapados*. We were very happy to be sleeping in that room.

'Maybe the slaves lived here hundreds of years ago?'

'Maybe we are going to see a flame coming out of the wall at night?'

We played all day long in the house, but somehow we always ended up in the living room to check the time with the big clock that was standing there. The day passed very slowly.

At the end of the day it was dark. It generally is at night. Jaime and I were on guard. I took the first four hours, and Jaime had to watch till the next morning.

I stayed awake for my watch like a good soldier. Then I fell asleep.

I heard Jaime telling me something in my dream. But it wasn't a dream. Jaime was sweating and shaking. 'Wake up! Wake up! I saw the fire in the wall!' He pointed to the direction and we started to work. We prepared a knife and an iron stick and started to make a hole in the wall.

We worked for an hour, and tried to be silent, so as not to wake anybody. The hole was going deeper and deeper. Jaime was bigger than I and he put his arm in . . . 'I found something! I'm touching it! It's still hot from the fire!'

When he pulled his arm out, he was holding a silver pitcher. It was still hot. It was the morning coffee from the kitchen next door.

The Aunt from Romania

Jaffa is one of the oldest cities in the world. According to Greek mythology, Joppa, daughter of Aeolos, God of the Winds, founded the place.

According to Jewish tradition, it is named after Japhet, Noah's son.

Mythology and tradition both accept the saga of a terrible monster. When Joppa's daughter Andromeda refused to marry Poseidon, the master of the sea sent an enormous monster to blockade Jaffa port, until Andromeda was delivered to be devoured.

The Bible has the prophet Jonah swallowed by a big fish after he had, against the will of God, embarked for Tarshish.

Dagon, the philistine fish-baal, who held sway in Jaffa, is also known as Joannas.

In Roman times, Vespasian destroyed Jaffa as a haunt of Jewish pirates. After so many destructions and conquests, not much of ancient Jaffa could possibly survive.

The names of Poseidon and Andromeda are remembered to this day. They are the names of restaurants.

Names like Jonah and the Jewish pirates have new bodies, the dealers of the flea market in Jaffa. To these names there are a few to add: Amos, David, Shlomo, Emil, Noah ...

Among the big conquests of Jaffa's flea market is the Polish one. I mean the first Polish Jewish dealers. They were followed by the Romanians, and the last ones to come were the Persians. In

Poland, Romania and Persia they were called Jews. In Israel they are called Romanian, Polish and Persian.

To be a good antique dealer you have to learn that profession at the flea market. That is the antique-dealing university. Dealers in Jaffa start backgammon early in the morning. That is, after a tour to see what people have brought for sale. With the morning coffee it starts. Little tables are outside the shops, surrounded by the experts.

In a flea market you can buy everything. People who look for a bargain generally get it.

Sometimes, in the Jaffa flea market, it was possible to buy good objects of art. The price of those objects was according to the dealer's feeling of what he had to sell, or the interest of the customer.

Sheinkin Street coffee house was no longer for antique dealers. The owner sold the place. It was just like magic. The place sold, a few dealers died . . . Today it is a place where you have a cup of coffee, that's all.

I graduated from Sheinkin Street with very good marks. Now I was ready for the university. The flea market.

Stories of the objects that people saw in houses were endless. I used to hear at least two of them a day. I still do. Sometimes the stories were true, and I was able to buy very good artifacts.

Arieh B. was a dealer at the flea market. He used to sell old furniture that he bought from old ladies who went into old-people's homes. Most of these items, tables, chairs, etc., were very good because they belonged to people who came from Germany in 1933 and brought their goods with them. They were the lucky ones.

That was a very good time for the flea market and collectors. Children of those old people wanted to be modern. Today it has changed: to be modern is to have antiques.

It was an early morning when Arieh B. told me he had an address. It was an old aunt from Romania, who had brought with her two very large crates full of Jewish religious objects. At the beginning, I thought that it was just another morning story, but when he showed a Hanuka menorah I was very surprised. It was a museum piece. The price was very high, but still, as a good antique dealer, it was a prestige piece, so that even if I didn't make any profit, or only a very small one, it was important to have it.

Two days later, Arieh B. told me that the old lady decided to sell two more pieces. My surprise was even greater. This time it was another Hanukah lamp and a pair of antique candlesticks. The price again was very high. It was actually the price that I should be asking, but again, I bought them.

Collectors and dealers were very happy. I was not the only one who was buying museum pieces at top prices; others were doing the same thing.

A few days later Arieh B. showed some more pieces. The aunt from Romania needed money again. She was giving all that money to her relatives. 'Very good,' Arieh B. said. I bought a few other objects, but could not sell them because local collectors purchased as well.

Very proudly I displayed the beautiful collection I bought from Arieh B. and from another dealer, who also purchased from Arieh B. They were real museum pieces.

A few months later I was still hearing from people who were buying Judaica from the aunt from Romania. I did not buy any more; I could not afford it.

Early one morning I started to open the gallery. My first customers were four detectives: 'Whatever you bought from Arieh B. is stolen . . .'

I did not believe what I was told. I saw the court's warrant. We took all the pieces to the police station. When we arrived at the precinct, it seemed that it was a congress of antique dealers and collectors. Everybody was there. Most of us had to spend a night in jail – we had a lot to talk about.

Every one of us was so ashamed and our pride was hurt. We, who had heard so many stories, and never believed them. One story we did believe, all of us: the story of the aunt from Romania. But we were not mistaken about the quality of the pieces. They were museum pieces. They were stolen from the museum.

The Wooden Cross

'Do not ever forget that you are a Jew, because if you do somebody is going to remind you.' Those were the words my grandfather used to say so many times. Even now, I can hear the sound of his voice.

I started my primary school at the age of five. No, I was not a genius. I was born in October, so I gained a year. Soriano and Soria were my best friends. We lived one house next to another. We sat in Grade 'A' at the same desk.

After the six years in primary school, I had to change schools. Soriano, Soria and I were very sorry we had to part. When the first day of secondary school started, I saw Soriano and Soria in the same classroom. They raised hell at home, and succeeded in changing schools too.

We were very good friends. We studied together, played together, and fought together. As we grew older and had an interest in the same girls, more than once one of us had a black eye. We were called the Three Musketeers. There was never a day that we were not together. Apart, that is, from the exceptions: Rosh Hashanah and Yom Kippur. The Jewish holydays.

Soria and Soriano were Roman Catholics. Almost all the inhabitants of Bolivia are. It is the national religion.

About Judaism very little was known, and sometimes ignorance is the mother of anti-Semitic feeling. It's because we Jews are different. It took a very long time, and much observation, before Soria and Soriano were convinced that we Jews don't kill little children for Passover; that it was only a Jewish religious festival commemorating the liberation of the Jews from slavery in Egypt.

They believed that we Jews killed Jesus, but that no one from my family or my ancestors had anything to do with it. I was their best friend. I never suffered from anti-Semitic comments.

Until the age of thirteen I was, for them, a German, because I was born in Germany. There was great admiration in Bolivia for everything that was German. The beer was German. The army had the German training system. The uniforms were in the German style. Bolivia was also the shelter of many war criminals.

The Sorias and Sorianos were two families that had lived for centuries in Bolivia. It is said they came with the *conquistadores*, with Pizarro and Mendoza.

As members of those very old families, their original home was Sucre and Tarija. These two cities were the haven of the noble families in Bolivia.

Soria and Soriano were very interested when I studied Hebrew for my *barmitzvah*; now they were more convinced than ever that everything that we Jews did was different; we even read and write from right to left.

The biggest fights we had were when I used to tell them that actually many Bolivian families are from Jewish origins, because they escaped from Spain to the New World. Only then I felt anti-semitism.

'We are Christians, we are Roman Catholics! How dare you say that!'

'I'm sorry, I did not mean it.' I did mean it, but I did not want to lose my friends.

Years later I was in Soria's house. It was a very old house. A colonial house. At the entrance was a very big wooden cross. Soria told me that the cross came from Spain. Maybe not, but it looked very old.

Even years before, when I saw the cross, I was always very curious as to why it was made that way. The cross was very big and very simple. It was carved from a very large piece of wood. What was unusual was the junction of the cross. Somehow it did not fit. It was too big.

For many years I did not dare to ask about it. Especially because, every time they entered that big room, with great reverence, they made the sign of the cross.

That junction was like a box. One day we were alone in the house. We were talking about the paintings that were hanging on the walls. They were very old ones, and similar to the ones we saw in the museum. Many of those paintings were in books of colonial art. They were the pride of the family.

I asked my friend, 'Do you think that there is something inside the junction of the cross?'

'No, I don't think so. Do you think there should be something?'

'It looks like a box.'

'It is not a box. I am sure of it. Did you ever see a cross with a box in the middle?'

'No.' We were looking at the cross for some time. Soria brought a chair. He stood on the chair to get a closer look. When I stood on the chair I was sure that there was something inside the cross.

'Could we bring the cross down?'

'Let's not speak about the cross any more. It is blasphemy.'

'No, it is not blasphemy. It is nothing against your god. The cross is an object.'

'The cross is holy. Maybe because you are a Jew it is just an object for you.'

'Of course it is a religious object. I agree to that, I respect your belief and you should respect mine.'

Soria calmed down. We left the room and went to the patio. It was a beautiful place. We were still thinking about the cross. Soria looked at me very seriously and said, 'OK, we take it down. We'll do it very carefully. But if there is nothing in that junction I'll make you pay for it.'

We had the big cross lying on the big table. Now it was even bigger and heavier than it was on the wall. We started to look at the junction. It actually was like a box. When we started to knock it, it sounded hollow. We did not know where the opening was. Then Soria said he'd found it. A little piece of wood moved.

And then it came out. Inside was a parchment. It was a *mezuzah*. It was handwritten and still very well preserved.

'It is a *mezuzah*.'

'What is a *mezuzah*?'

I tried to explain that a *mezuzah* is the first commandment that a Jew is enjoined by the Torah to fulfil, by affixing it on the doorpost at the entrance. I told him to look in the Bible. He brought one.

We opened it at Deuteronomy. The holy name was written on the *mezuzah* and also the Hebrew word *shadai*, the sacramental name of God.

We put the cross back on the wall. The parchment was inside again. When the members of the family would return they would make the sign of the cross with reverence. Soria made me promise not to say what we had found inside.

Can the God of Israel ever forgive me that I did not keep that promise?

The Pendulum

One of the biggest experiences that an antique dealer goes through is to see how his customer checks what he is buying.

The questions customers ask are sometimes difficult to answer, so with the years an antique dealer has his own official answers. I have mine.

'Where did you get all this?'

'My grandfather was a pirate . . . He left me a map . . .' People think whatever they want to, if they do not accept the answer of the pirate:

'Every Monday afternoon I go to Moishe Zimmerman. He lives on Allenby Street, Number 178, second floor. You have to ring twice. He sells only to people his father approves.'

'How do I know that this is an antique?'

'Once I went to my physician. I had a pain in the lower part of my left side. I asked him what I had. He replied, after checking, "My dear fellow, you have appendicitis." "Doctor, how do I know that I have that?" "You have two ways of knowing. The first, you go to a medical school for seven years, then you specialize in internal medicine for another five. After that you need a few years of experience. What is the other? You take my word." I took his word. You know what I had? Appendicitis.'

In olden times people used to bite coins to check if they were real gold or silver. I know people who would do it these days.

There are customers who love to wet archaeological objects. Sometimes they take them to their mouths and then smell them.

It must be a very good ancient system, but we still don't know how it works.

To bring a piece to the light and make a very thoughtful face helps to identify the period.

People love very difficult names, if they want to buy something to impress their friends. With an ancient pottery jug, they like to be able to say, 'It is a zoophite ritual mystic vessel from the late Chalcolithic Early Bronze period.'

Some people are more sophisticated. They come in equipped with a magnifying glass. They start to check the artifact all over, trying to find something to catch their eye. Generally, after a long check, it is the price tag they discover. It is the only thing they don't like.

Some people have to check with their chequebook and others have to check with their wives.

Collectors are divided into two categories: those who love the items they collect, and others who are in eternal competition with other collectors, the ones who have accumulated the biggest, the most important, the rarest and so on. Antique dealers love the others more.

Art and antique collectors are also people who would see an inexpensive artifact and would not buy it because it is cheap. The appreciation comes with the price. Ignorance is also a very good seller. People don't want to say they don't know or understand. If the dealers ask if he ever heard the name of an artist, or a certain culture, the answer will be, immediately, yes. That is after the dealer has sold the piece.

Amongst collectors are those who fall in love with everything. 'Oh, I love it!' 'Oh, this is exactly what I was looking for.' 'Oh, isn't it gorgeous!' When an antique dealer hears those wonderful expressions about his antiques, the answer is very simple: no sale. The expressions of admiration themselves are the payment.

Thousands of people would not visit an art or antique gallery if they had to pay an entrance fee, but on the other hand, for many people it is the discovery of a new world.

Some people want to belong to the world of collectors, the world of art, but the only thing they have is money. Some even think that culture can be bought in the supermarket.

Culture is something that you are born with or grow up with. It is called, in German, *Kinderstube*.

Children are the best connoisseurs. They have very good eyes for antiques. No wonder they also know how to choose the best toys.

If a lonely man buys a piece of antique jewellery, it is not for his wife. But if a lonely woman buys a piece of men's jewellery, then the chances are that it is for her husband.

The very special people who buy art and antiques are the ones who love the pieces they buy. Some of them build a house around a piece of art as some people build a life around a person.

Luck and magic are also important factors in antique dealing.

She came back. The woman with the pendulum.

A pendulum is a weight attached to a line. It has been known for thousands of years. It is to build straight. To erect walls. It is probably the only thing in this world that is straight. It shows correctness. If it does show correctness in the practical things in life, for many people it is also for the soul or the heart.

The plummet and the pendulum are the same. I call the pendulum a practical instrument to be used for emotional objectives.

In some countries, a woman who was about to give birth was laid on a bed. A small pendulum of copper was hung on a string above her belly. An old woman was the one who held the pendulum. If it started to move in a round movement it was a sign that a boy was to be born. If the movement was straight, from one side to another, a girl was on her way into this world.

In love stories, the pendulum had a major role. Women used it over the pictures of the men they loved. If the pendulum started to move from left to right, love was there for ever; if it was the opposite, it was a dangerous love, and, if it stood still, no love at all.

The pendulum was also used on the zodiac signs. The *zodiakos kuklos*, meaning the circle of figures in the zodiac, had to be under the pendulum; that way it was decided who was the person, from the zodiac symbol, who had to be chosen.

She was back with her pendulum. I never knew if she was going to buy something until she chose something she loved, until she checked the piece with her pendulum.

She took the artifact and sat at my desk. It was unbelievable to see such a beautiful woman taking her pendulum out from her purse. It was a little leather bag. It was a very small copper one hanging on a thin line. Her long blonde hair fell forward, over her face and shoulders. The little pendulum started moving round in circles. She stopped the pendulum and asked it again. The same movement. The final approval.

The Inheritance

On the eve of the festival big crowds convene in Safed from all parts of Israel. Ashkenazi and Sephardi Jews attend the pilgrimage. Yemenite Jews are there too. Jews take part in the celebrations which are the revival of ancient rites in Israel.

All afternoon a great procession, carrying the Torah scrolls, winds through the alleys and lanes of picturesque Safed. There is singing and dancing on every corner.

In the evening people rush to Mount Meiron. They all have to be there. Just before nightfall, the celebration starts with prayers. All are now near, or in the tomb of Shimon Bar Yochai. Jews, obsessed by demons, are exorcized dancing; sometimes they even knock their heads against the walls. All this under the light of thousands of burning candles. That is the night one can believe in the legend of the priests from Jerusalem who fled the temple and continued the sacrificial cult now in Safed.

That night everybody was happy. But in Shimon's house they were sad. Shimon was going to die. They all surrounded his bed. The whole family. They were not rich, and the old man started to talk: 'The house belongs to all, so there will not be a problem.'

Each of the members of the family moved closer to the bed.

'The *Kiddush** cup, that belonged to my grandfather, may

* Sanctification.

he rest in peace, will be for Shlomo. The *Hanukiah**, I mean the one we also used in Jerusalem outdoors, is going to be for David.' The young men started to look at each other. They were used to those religious objects, and now every one of them wanted each object for himself.

'*Sifrei Kodesh*, the religious books. The *Gemarah*† for you, Joseph. The *Humashim*†, the Torah books, for Benjamin.'

The daughters were standing behind the mother; they were weeping.

'The old map on the wall is for you, Hannah. It is very precious. It is one of the oldest maps of the Holy Land. For you, Sarah, a book; it is a very old one. It is the first that was printed in the Holy Land, here in Safed, in 1575. The rest stays with your mother, till one hundred and twenty‡.' The man closed his eyes, and went to God, smiling.

The young men were shocked. Their father said nothing about the *Kushan*, the property document of the house in Jerusalem.

The girls had received valuable things, and the boys nothing but religious objects.

Jews refer to the cemetery as the house of life. It comes from the Bible. They brought the late Shimon to the cemetery. The sons said *Kaddish*. They mourned their father. They loved their father.

'He was always so just with all of us, I don't understand the reason he did not mention the other goods he had.'

'We are not rich and we need the money. We have to convince Hannah to sell the old map, and Sarah ...'

'Sarah will never sell the book!'

'I don't think that Hannah will sell her antique map either.'

'It is not hers! It is ours! Father was dying, he did not know what he was doing!'

'You are right. We are the men of the house. You are the elder brother; you have to decide.'

'I think that we don't have to ask. We just take everything that is for sale. And afterwards we give the girls their part.'

'What about mother?'

'She will not know. She is old. She does not need all that.'

---

* The branched candelabra for Hanukah.
† Religious books.
‡ A blessing for a long and healthy life.

'She does not know where the *Kushan* is. We lost everything.'

'But we cannot sell the religious objects.'

'Why not? They are ours. We are not religious. Father was.'

'These are old books; dealers pay a lot of money for them.'

'We can sell them, and buy new prints. It is the same. And we'll still have money in our pockets.'

'Yes, it is a good idea. Let's do it.'

'Let's go to the antique dealer in Jaffa. The one with the beard.'

They started going up the street of Old Jaffa. They passed the Great Mosque. The door was open. They saw the Roman columns in the mosque cloisters that were stolen from Ashkelon. The men passed the house of Simon, the tanner. The name Simon meant something.

'We have a few things for sale.'

'What are they?'

'We have old books, an old map, a *Kiddush* goblet and an old Hanukah lamp. Are you interested?'

'Yes.'

I saw the pieces that they brought. The map was an outstanding piece of art, the book a unique piece. All the other objects were rare as well. I asked their price, but the brothers wanted an offer. I generally did not offer, but this time I did.

'We think it is worth more.'

'Of course, otherwise I wouldn't be buying. This is exactly what I am here for, to make money.'

Somehow it was reasonable what I said. They agreed.

After they left I started cleaning the Hanukah lamp and the antique *Kiddush* goblet. They were beautiful. Later on, with more time, I started to look, page by page, at the old book. It was a collector's piece.

And the map. The map of the Holy Land. I started to examine it. I saw a coloured point on it, in Jerusalem. It should not be there. I started to open the old frame. I did not like it. I'll frame it with another wooden frame, I thought. But between the cardboard and the map was a document. A *Kushan*. It was the deed of sale of a house in Jerusalem. It had the government seal. It was a legal document.

I looked up and saw a woman in front of me.

'Would you sell all these things to me, these ... here on the table?'

'I just bought them.'

'I know, from my sons. I followed them. I have to take them back home. Shimon's home. I give you some profit, so . . .'

'I do not want to sell them right now.'

'I want to tell you a story. Can you give me a few minutes?'

'Yes.'

'It was in biblical times. There was a man who was called, let us say, Shimon. He had a very rare coin that he just bought, and paid very much for it. He invited his best friends to show them his new purchase, the very rare coin. It was evening and this Shimon showed the coin to his friends, while they were having supper. At that very same moment the lights went out and the coin disappeared. Shimon asked his friends to give him back the coin. Nobody answered. He asked again and the answer was the same. He said to them, "If you don't give me my coin I shall search your pockets." Since there was no answer, he started to do so.

'One by one he searched them. There was a friend of his – let's call him Joseph. Joseph said, "If I have your coin, let it be that something bad should happen to my family."

'A few moments later came into the house a man who told Joseph that his house had collapsed and that he had lost his family.

'Shimon and his friends held the man, Joseph. Shimon put his hand in Joseph's pocket and took out a coin. Shimon said it was his. All his friends saw it. Joseph was taken out into the street and stoned to death.

'This is not the end of the story. A few months later, Shimon was cleaning his house for Passover. Between the stones of his floor he found his coin. Joseph had a coin too. He did not want to lose it. The things you have here are my coin. I do not want to lose them.

'Today my children did not understand the inheritance their father left. Maybe they will understand mine.

The Little Torah

A certain family had a collection of Jewish ceremonial art. It was not the biggest collection known, but it was a very good one. The religious objects passed from one generation to another. Every generation added a few pieces to the collection. Little children in the family knew every piece and its history.

There was a list, like a catalogue, where every object was recorded, and even from where it was bought, and how much was paid for it.

The Jewish community in Breslau exhibited the collection and a little catalogue was published. Two years later the collection was exhibited in Berlin. This was shortly after the First World War.

The head of the family was my grandfather. He had just returned from the war. He came from the front with three things: first, his Iron Cross decoration; second, an iron watch chain. (He gave his gold one in exchange. It had an inscription: 'In Eiserner Zeit 1916*'.) And third, typhoid.

In those four years my grandmother produced soap, to support the family. In the beginning she sold some goods, but the collection was not touched.

The years passed; a few items were added to the collection. In 1933 a new Germany was born. At first nobody realized that it was not a new Germany, but the biggest killing machine mankind has ever known.

* During the War, 1916.

My grandfather took the collection to a very dear friend of his, in the hope that some day those Jewish ceremonial objects would be in the family again. We were allowed to leave Germany with ten marks in our pockets. The personal jewellery was given to the Nazis. Sometimes people received a receipt. We got one. So we left Germany with ten marks and with our lives.

The stories of the collection and its objects I had heard so many times that I even could visualize them.

Silver spice boxes, Hanukah lamps, Purim *megillas*, books and so on. At the end, my grandfather used to talk about the Little Torah. It was a miniature scroll, the handles of which were made of gold-plated silver. The finials were made of ivory, very ornate.

'Do you think that one day you are going to find that friend and get everything back?'

'You can never know, my son. Strange things do happen.'

'It would be wonderful to see all that splendour.'

It was very difficult to imagine such a wonderful collection and, at the same time, not to know if there was enough food for the next day. But dreams are very cheap; even poor people can afford them.

It was Hanukah when my grandfather found the old catalogue from the exhibition in Breslau. He explained every piece that was photographed and, in even more detail, the objects that were not.

'You see, this is an Italian Torah pointer, from Naples. This pointer is unusual, because of the spice section included above the hand. It is pierced for the aroma that comes out while reading the Torah.'

'What is this?'

'This is a silver-cased Esther scroll, from Prague. Today it would be a hundred and eighty years old.'

'This is a Hanukah lamp!' I said – eager to show that I knew something.

'Yes, but not a regular one. This one was from the eighteenth century. It had inside a musical box, with the melody of Maoz Tzur. But this is the Little Torah. That Little Torah was with our family for over two hundred years.' That was the first time I saw my grandfather with tears in his eyes.

To hold that catalogue was like holding a treasure. I knew it belonged to us. It made me feel rich.

The Nazis robbed the Jews. The Communists robbed the

Nazis. My grandfather's friend probably had died, and the collection was gone.

An antique dealer is rich if he has books. The books give knowledge, and knowledge is something that nobody can take away. Nobody can steal it. It is untouchable. Knowledge is like conscience; they are the same size. They are so small that when you have them they are hardly noticed, but if you don't they jump out.

Looking through catalogues is fun. Every time it is a new discovery. I had one in my hands when I saw a Little Torah that was once on exhibition in New York. It looked like the same Torah my grandfather had. I found the old catalogue my grandfather left me, and began to compare the two Torahs. Every detail was exact. The Little Torah's embroidered cover was the last proof I needed. It had the same inscription. The Little Torah was back.

I contacted the institution which exhibited it and I was told that it belonged to a collector whom I shall call Kalkalsky.

The redemption of the first-born is performed in accordance with the tradition that began in Egypt. When the Israelites left Egypt, all the first-born were sanctified to God. Five silver shekels were given to redeem the first-born. When a father declares that he wishes to redeem his son, he gives the priest five silver coins. The priest accepts the coins and announces that the child is redeemed. I had to redeem the Little Torah.

'I would like to buy the Little Torah you have. You see, it belonged to my family. You have here some other objects that belonged to my family's collection. I would also like to buy them.'

'These objects are not for sale. I bought them after the war, and I have no intention of selling them.'

'But they belonged to my family. Does that mean nothing?'

'Every antique sometime belonged to someone. Now they belong to me.'

'Here, please look at this old catalogue. You see, here is the Little Torah, and here is the Torah pointer.'

'I am not selling!'

It was a rainy Friday in New York. I left Kalkalsky's home very sad. What could I do? The man said he bought the pieces. After so many years, who knows through how many hands those ceremonial objects had passed.

Saturday morning. I was in the synagogue. It is a very beautiful custom that, when a visitor comes to the synagogue on *shabbat*, he is called to the Torah. I was called. While I was saying the specified benediction to read that chapter, I saw my grandfather's eyes. I saw the tears. I was sad.

The cantor started with the *mussaf*, the prayer after reading the

Torah. I was seated next to an elderly man who noticed my sadness. He invited me to his home, for *Kiddush*.

I don't know why, but I told him the story. The collection. The Torah . . . Kalkalsky. I wanted to buy the ceremonial objects back. I wanted to redeem them.

The man gave me his card. He said that he was going to help me. He asked me to call him on Monday. I took his card and read his name. He was a judge.

I said goodbye and how grateful I was for his offer. I told him that I would pay anything the man wanted, even if I had to work many years to pay it.

When Jacob had his dream and saw the ladder going to the sky, it says in the Torah that the angels go up and the angels come down. If the angels go up first that means that the angels are here with us; and the ones who come down are changing guard with the angels who are going up.

When I called the judge on Monday he asked me to come over to his chambers. Kalkalsky was there. The judge said that Kalkalsky was willing to sell the Little Torah and the Hanukah lamp. He named a price. I agreed. Friends helped me to pay the amount. It was 'redemption' day. Like the day that the Torah was given to Israel. The Little Torah was home again.

The Cameo

People used to say that her late husband was the biggest tomb robber of our time. If it was true, then most of the missing statues from Cesaria and Ashkelon that appeared in the world market were from his collection.

It was said that sometimes the Roman sculptures were so big that he simply used to cut them in pieces. So many things were said about this man that it was a legend. A legend, yes, when you heard the stories. A thrilling mixture of admiration and disgust when you saw the pieces in sales catalogues stating: 'From the Fahat collection'.

The Fahat collection was endless. Almost in every sale, in the big auction houses, are offered the finest artifacts from the Herodian period.

Jericho, in the course of five thousand years, has changed its location. The spring of Elisha, in the Bible, was revived, after the Babylonian return of the Jews, as a little village.

Herod the Great constructed a new city within a fortress. It is said he was buried there. Herod was the biggest builder Israel had. His buildings were very expensive. Herod needed the means for it. He had a bank. He looted King David's tomb. He was a tomb robber.

. . . Then they turned to the task of the king's burial. Everything possible was done by Archealus to add to the magnificence: he brought out all the royal ornaments to be carried in procession in honour of the dead monarch. There was a solid gold bier, adorned with precious stones and draped with the richest purple. On it lay the body wrapped in crimson, with a diadem resting on the head and above that a golden crown, and the sceptre by the right hand. The bier was escorted by Herod's sons ... The body was borne twenty-four miles to Herodium, where, at the late king's command, it was buried. So ends the story of Herod.

Archaeologists, collectors and dealers read the above lines from Flavius Josephus, and tried to find Herod's tomb. 'So ends the story of Herod ... ', and thus begins the story of Fahat.

Fahat was the only one who possessed unique Herodian pieces. Other dealers had only artifacts from the Herodian period. Dealers used to follow Fahat trying to find out his source. They failed. Government officials failed, too. Then Fahat died, and his secret went with him.

The widow, Madam Fahat, lived in Florence, in a little palace. She was in her early sixties but she looked much younger. She was a beautiful woman, carbon-black hair, big brown eyes and a very good figure. She was a very proud woman, and known as the best-dressed woman of her time. Everything she wore was black. She wore in the mornings what other women used to wear at big dance parties. When she passed through the streets of Florence, people looked at her with respect and admiration. There was always a young good-looking man next to her, it was said, to protect her.

She wore only one piece of jewellery, a gold pendant. A cameo. It was unique. Rumour had it that the pendant had belonged to King Herod the Great. It was comparable only with the most famous of the cameos of all classical gems. The *Gemma Augustae*, showing Tiberius in triumph preceding Augustus and Roma.

The widow's cameo was onyx and she wore it as if it were a medal received from the king himself.

The first time my wife saw her, she fell in love with the cameo. I used to buy from Mrs Fahat, from time to time, very good archaeological pieces. The price was always high, but it was worth it. She spoke excellent English.

At the end of every deal I used to ask her if she would consider selling that cameo.

'Mrs Fahat, you know it is not for business. It is for my wife.'

'Maybe some day, my friend, maybe some day . . . '

Mrs Fahat used to come, once a year, to Israel. She owned a house in Jericho, not very far from the Kallia Hotel, that does not exist any more. When we saw her in a car with her bodyguard, leaving Jerusalem in the direction of Jericho, I thought that maybe she might go to Herod's tomb.

We passed the excavation site of Tell-Jericho and Tel-es-Sultan. At Khirbet Rahab we lost her.

'She is probably in her house now.'

'Every time she comes to the country she has more antiquities for sale. She must have them in some place.'

'Yes, but where?'

'I think that when God started to give brains to people, she cried out twice, "I am here," and she got a double portion.'

A few days later she called me and offered a few antiquities for sale . . .

Every year it was the same story. Every year there were new offers of artifacts. Ancient gold jewellery, glass and pottery. The ancient coins that she offered indicated the period. It was the period of King Herod the Great.

'I would still like to buy your cameo.'

'You know, my dear friend, I am getting old. I promise you that one day this cameo is going to be yours. One day your wife is going to be as happy wearing it as I was when I got it from my late husband.'

A year later Mrs Fahat did not come. I started to ask about her, and I was told she was ill. I decided to go to Florence and meet her; it was also an opportunity to see that beautiful city. When I arrived at her little palace, people dressed in black were standing outside. A black hearse was waiting. I understood that I was too late.

The coffin was carried out by four men. Behind the coffin was the young man who was with her on her last visit to the Holy Land. The young man approached me: 'I would like to meet you after the ceremony.'

We all followed the car. She was buried in her little palace courtyard.

'It is good you are here,' said the young man, 'You have saved me a trip to your country. Here, I have an envelope for you.' I

116

knew what it was. It was the cameo. There was also a little note: 'My dear friend, as you see I kept my promise. This is also the bill for the cameo and its gold chain. Maybe we'll do some business in the next world. In heaven they need antique dealers too. You know, there must be antiques there, too.'

The price was very high, but it was worth it.

Some people say that if King Herod robbed King David's tomb, there was no reason why his too shouldn't be robbed. One day, archaeologists will find the tomb of King Herod the Great. And digging ten metres down, they will find a visiting card: 'King Fahat was here . . . '

Marie Antoinette

At the foot of Mount Carmel there always existed two cities. They were twin cities. Salmona, a very small port in the lee of the mountain, and Sycamion, the village that supplied food and goods to the people and ships of Salmona. Sycamion was no more after the Arab conquest, and Salmona is known today as Haifa.

In the year 1898, Haifa had two great visitors, Theodor Herzel and the German Kaiser, Wilhelm II.

Herzel said that Haifa was the city of the future. He was right.

Maria Theresa was the queen of Hungary and Bohemia. Her right to the throne was contested and gave rise to the war of the Austrian succession. Marie Antoinette was the daughter of Maria Theresa. She was guillotined after the French Revolution.

Eva Grosz lived in Haifa. She was called Marie Antoinette. She even had some papers to prove that she was from the royal family. She called herself Marie Antoinette the Second. She had a very good reason for this.

Her home was a very big room, surrounded with French furniture. All from the period of Marie Antoinette. On the walls were paintings from the eighteenth and nineteenth centuries. It was not the case of a painting hanging here and there. There were so many paintings that it was impossible to see the wall.

She had everything in that room; it was just like a museum. Showcases all over, silverware, porcelain figurines – Meissen, Lalique, Galle, Faience, Capo di Monte . . .

In the middle of the room was her big bed. It was covered with a big curtain that fell at the sides, with many pillows all over. She always lay on the bed, and her visitors had to sit around the bed.

Her dress was always silk and the colour rose was her favourite.

People used to come to her from abroad. She was a tourist attraction. They heard the story of the princess. The princess, Marie Antoinette.

Twenty-five years ago, she was already old. Maybe eighty or a little less. Nobody knew her age, but it was not important. Nobody needed to know.

She was always in need of money, so to her sorrow she had to sell paintings that belonged to the royal family.

She had papers, very old ones, that were written in a language that was difficult to read and understand, to show that she belonged to the family of Marie Antoinette. She had blue blood in her veins.

Whenever she spoke, it was half in Hungarian and half in French. It had to be. It belonged to her roots.

When she showed the papers they were so overwhelming that nobody actually looked at them, they just listened to her explanations. She was very convincing: 'You see, this is the document . . . ' All the papers she ever showed had seals printed in wax, and if somebody wanted to try to read what was written, she would always say, 'You will have to come some other day, with more time . . . '

Collectors from all over the country used to come to her house. It was a privilege if the princess would sell something. You had to convince her that whatever was bought from her was going into good hands, and would be treasured. Sometimes it took over an hour to try to convince Marie Antoinette that it was actually all right for the customer to have the painting. At that moment she would decide the price. It was not only the price of the painting, it was also to compensate her for her suffering in parting from that piece of art. Not only that, but it was part of her family and her life, it was just like parting from a son. That was part of the price.

So the *nouveau riche* of Haifa had something new in their homes. Something that had belonged to the royal family. Every painting was a conversation piece. Every Friday night it was the general conversation of who had bought what from Marie Antoinette.

If the *nouveau riche* of Haifa had royal objects, then the *nouveau riche* of Jerusalem and Tel-Aviv could not be far behind . . .

Every day new cars were parking in front of Marie Antoinette's house. The police even had problems with the traffic.

The old lady, the last member of the royal family, maybe the great-niece of Maria Theresa, had to sell her property. She had not enough to pay the local taxes.

It was a rule that nobody could buy anything the very same day. She needed some time to part with the pieces she sold. People had to wait for days, and sometimes weeks, until they received their objects. When the objects were handed over, the princess always had tears in her eyes. Her heart was broken, but after a while she used to smile: 'If it is in your hands, I am very happy.'

Jean Ferdinand was a young Frenchman who used to help her. He was the one who prepared the tea. He always offered different types of tea: English, Indian, mixed . . . I tasted them all. They were all the same.

For over twenty years Marie Antoinette sold her goods, and whenever I visited her it seemed to be that she had the supply of the Louvre Museum. It was endless.

She was invited to every official party and was very active in public services. Her pictures were always in the newspapers. It was always the same story. The last princess. Like Anastasia. The poor woman.

Farkash had a little antique shop in Haifa. He collected everything and his speciality was collecting women. It was said that he was an art and antique dealer in Hungary. He had a very large selection of antique paintings which he used to buy from the residents of old-people's homes. Since in the old days photography had not yet been invented, people used to order portraits of members of their families. These portraits of people always bore some resemblance to other people from those times. Farkash had many books with pictures of famous people or royal families, and he was an expert in touching up his old portraits to look like other personalities.

Once I wanted to buy a painting from him. He said that it was not for sale. He had received the painting for restoration. Later on, I saw the painting at Marie Antoinette's home. A year later or so, the same story.

A few months later, I was with another dealer at an old-people's home. We saw some old paintings, family portraits belonging to one of the residents. We bought some silverware.

I did not know at that time that those paintings were destined to be royal figures from the family of Maria Theresa, queen of Hungary, the mother of Marie Antoinette, queen of Louis xvi, and the ancestor of Eva Grosz, from the city of Sycamion, known today as Haifa.

A Letter from a Cousin

Ever since the creation of the State of Israel we have had, in our landscape, United Nations officers. They were here because somebody sent them over. It is said that they are the peace-keepers. They have tried very hard to do their jobs. We Israelis did not invite them. We did not invite wars either.

I don't know how much they succeeded in their jobs as peace-keepers. What I do know is that some of them were the finest and biggest antiquities smugglers of all time.

Since 1948 the traffic of artifacts was in the hands of the UN officers, as there were no relations between Israel and the border-ing Arab countries.

Officers who finished their stay in the area made sure that the newcomers would understand that antiquities are more appreci-ated here than in Jordan or in Syria.

In the early sixties the first commercial Arab–Israeli agreements were sealed. It was not official, and politics had nothing to do with it. The wars meant nothing where business was concerned. It was profitable for all parties involved. 'A Jew never breaks the law; he just bends it a little.' This is an old saying. I don't know if it exists in Arabic, but I know that law-bending exists amongst Arabs too.

Mohamed Nasser el-Din and I met for the first time in 1967, in Hebron. It was the eighth day after the Six Day War. We were not strangers; we had done some business before, but only by correspondence. He used to send ancient glass, coins and pottery through the mail. The mail was a UN officer from Sweden.

There were many Arab dealers from Jerusalem, Bethlehem and Ramalah who used to export antiquities the same way to Jewish dealers in Jerusalem and Tel-Aviv. Nasrallah was one of them. He was a real expert. He was also one of the very few who knew that Jewish antiquities were the best for the Jews.

The best price for an American coin is in America. The best price for a Peruvian stamp is in Peru. The best price for a Jewish object is all over the world. Jews are all over the world.

'Nasrallah sends you his best wishes. He also sends these Jewish coins from the first revolt. Here, you see, are three silver shekels.'

'Thank you very much. Is there something else?'

'Yes, he said that he had something written in Hebrew, or something that looks like Hebrew . . . '

'May I see it?'

'I don't have it with me. He said that it is expensive.'

'Give Nasrallah my best wishes and tell him that in any case he should send it with you. If I do not have the money to buy it, I'll have somebody who does.'

The Swedish officer jumped on his UN jeep and waved goodbye. The UN flag waved goodbye too.

'I'll see you on my next leave!'

'My regards to King Hussein!'

Three months later the Swede was back. Among pottery vessels, coins and ancient glass, he had a little piece of parchment . . .

Early one morning in 1947, a Bedouin shepherd, searching for a stray goat, entered a cave situated in Qumran, next to the Dead Sea. He saw, lying there, some jars containing ancient manuscripts. He did not know that he had made the greatest discovery of our time: the Dead Sea Scrolls. He sold these scrolls to a shoemaker in Bethlehem, to be used as material to repair shoes, thus making him the most important antiquities dealer of modern times.

In the Qumran caves, the Essenes were the people who lived there for two hundred years. They considered themselves as the 'sons of light'; they were the elected ones, and the 'sons of darkness' were the rest of humanity.

'Nasrallah said that this is part of a letter, and since it is Jewish it should be from an old cousin of yours . . . '

'But this is not a letter. It is a fragment.'

'That is all that he gave me. So, see here. This is his note and you can see how much he wants for it.'

'Leave it with me, please. I am going to show it to somebody who might be interested.'

'If you don't buy it now, I have to bring it back to him. I am leaving this evening.'

I did not have the money. The situation reminded me of one when I was a child. I was standing with my grandfather: 'Do you see all this land in front of you?'

'Yes, grandfather.'

'Do you see all the land, left and right?'

'Yes, grandfather.'

'All that land we could have owned, if I would have given, for that piece of land, one pair of boots.'

'Why didn't you give the boots?'

'I didn't have a pair of boots.'

A year later, I found out that a Jerusalem dealer had bought two Bar Kochbah letters from the Dead Sea caves. He bought them in fragments. He made a fortune. They were letters from Bar Kochbah himself, directed to his brothers in the Galilea. Two letters from an old cousin. Bar Kochbah.

The Jerusalem dealer had the pair of boots.

A Birthday Present

The first time I saw him, I thought that he wanted to clean the show windows. He was wearing an old factory overall. He had a funny old hat, and his boots were too big for his feet.

His fingernails had black dirt under them, and his hands were calloused. It was clear that the man was a mechanic, or something like that.

'I don't understand anything about antiques. You see, I have no education. I would like to buy a birthday present for a young lady. She loves antique jewellery. She also knows and understands about the different periods and all that.'

'Is it for your girlfriend?'

'I wish so. I dream of it . . . '

'You know that antique jewellery is quite expensive. I do not think, perhaps, you . . . '

'Yes, I can afford it. I have saved money for this occasion.'

I started to show him nice little pieces of antique jewellery, and I saw his thin face moving from one piece to another. His eyes were checking every detail. It looked as if he were trying to see the tiny parts of a motor.

'Why don't you show me something better? Maybe something bigger. Are you afraid of me? I am not a thief.' I did not answer. I did not want to offend him. I went to the place where I had more jewellery. I showed him an antique diamond pendant with a sapphire centre.

'This is very beautiful. I think it will please her. How much is it?'

I told him the price. He looked at the piece for a long time. I thought that he was going to say, thank you, but it is not for me. Instead: 'Can you put it in a nice box, and wrap it up as a birthday present?'

'Yes, I can do that.'

He started pulling out money bills from all his pockets. They were all of very low value. He started putting them in order, one after another. He counted the amount several times.

'Here, can you check it please. I am not very good at this.'

'It is all right. I counted it with you. Happy birthday!'

'Thank you.'

I was happy. Somehow I wanted the man to be happy too, so I did not charge him the full price. He did not know, but I made a big reduction.

It was February when I saw him again. He entered the gallery and went directly to the jewellery table.

'I need a birthday present. It has to be something special.'

'Is it for your girl from last year?'

'She is not my girlfriend yet, but I think . . . maybe this week . . .'

'Maybe you want a ring. Look at this, it is a very nice one. It is Victorian and it will go very well with the pendant of last year.'

'She loved the pendant. She said she is going to wear it when we go to the theatre.' He started to examine the ring. He put it on his finger, and smiled: 'My hands are not for rings, you know. They are oily.' He started to clean the ring by rubbing it on his overall.

'I think I am going to buy it for her. You know, she is very beautiful. She is very educated. She reads books and knows about classical music. She knows everything. Can you wrap it in a nice box?'

So many strange things happen in this world that maybe I should not be surprised by what a very cultured person had in common with that very simple soul. He probably did not buy a shirt for himself, and here he was, buying an exclusive antique jewellery piece.

At first I did not recognize him. I was there, waiting for my car to

be repaired. The mechanic could not find the reason for the strange noise my car made. He said that I had to leave the car for a day or two, to be examined. The man with the oily overall came over. He started checking the engine. He took a screwdriver, and two minutes later he smiled: 'Your car is OK. Nothing happened. See you again in February.'

'Did you go to the theatre with your girlfriend?'

'Not yet. You see, I am not ready for it yet.'

'What do you mean, you are not ready! Everybody goes to the theatre. The only thing you need is a ticket. That is all.'

'I cannot explain, but I am not ready yet.'

February came round again. The man was back for his birthday present. Somehow he looked much older than last year. He looked very tired.

'I would like a birthday present. I wrote it down. I mean the name.' He took out from the same overall a little piece of paper and started reading: 'Tiffany, yes, Tiffany. She would like a piece of Tiffany jewellery. Do you have any?'

'Yes.'

'Please excuse me, but what is Tiffany?' I explained to him the works of Tiffany in the nineteenth century. The lamps. The jewellery. The period. The so-called Art Nouveau. He was amazed. He took his newspaper and put it on the chair and sat down on it. I had to repeat it again. His thirst for knowledge was immense. He sat for two hours hearing my explanations. I showed him the books, and details of other artists from the same period. He took his little pencil and wrote down the names, the dates.

'I have to be honest with you. I don't have all the money this time. You see, I had expenses these last months. The girl wanted to paint her apartment and she needed a few new things. You know how things are.'

'Are you living with your girlfriend now?'

'No, she is not my girlfriend yet. She said that I am not ready yet. She is helping me. She is educating me. I see her once a week. She is very busy. You see, she has to read a lot. She also writes poems. She has already written two for me.'

'Are you sure that she is the girl for you?'

'Oh yes. She even said so. It is only a question of time. She is working very hard on my education.'

'It is all right, you can pay the rest later. I trust you.'

'Can you wrap it in a nice box, for her birthday?'

'Yes, as usual.'

A year later the man had grey hair already. He looked much older than he really was. His eyes were so sad that it pained me to look at them.

'It is her birthday. She wants an antique piece of Cartier. You know, a piece of jewellery. All that antique jewellery suits her so well. It looks as if she was born with it. Do you have it?'

'Yes, here I have a brooch–pendant in the form of a crescent with cushion-shaped diamonds, graduating in size.'

'I think she is going to love it. I saved money during the year. She looks like a princess with all that jewellery. Every time I see her, she says that she wants to be beautiful for me. She wrote a new poem for me.'

'Is she going to marry you?'

'She said that when I am ready, we are going to be married.'

I wrapped up the brooch–pendant for the birthday present.

Three months later I was in the garage. My old car had to be repaired again. I saw the death notice on the wall. I recognized the name.

'He was very ill. He died three days ago. His illness was love.'

Six months later, a tall beautiful woman entered the gallery.

'I have some very fine jewellery to sell. Tiffany and Cartier. It belonged to the family. Are you interested?'

'Yes.'

She opened the box and put the jewellery on the table, her elegant white hands arranging the pieces carefully. And I saw before me the dirty fingernails, the oily, calloused hands that had once held those birthday presents, before . . .

A Vase for a Flower

They were a very strange couple. They collected everything. Everyone saw them on the streets picking up everything that lay there. They always carried big bags on their shoulders. They were in their sixties, and were garbage collectors. It was a funny scene. Even in the very hot summers of Israel, they wore coats. Old raincoats. Her head was covered with a dirty old shawl and his with a very old rabbi's hat. They checked every dustbin, and saved whatever people used to throw away.

They lived in Beer-Sheba in one of the old houses. That was the place where they piled up their collection. The collection was so big that they had to sleep on it. The bed was covered with big bags and they had to step on bags to enter their home.

They were beggars, and they were known as crazy. People said it was because of the war. When they bent to pick up something and the raincoat did not cover their arms, a tattooed number with a little triangle could be seen.

The strange couple started to collect very early in the morning. They worked like little ants all day long, until the evening. They used to talk to each other, but if someone tried to listen they only heard noises.

When the Beer-Sheba sun used to say goodnight, the old woman used to enter one of the gardens and pick a flower. That was the sign that her collecting day was over.

The strange couple lived next to an archaeological site. The days after the first rain were the best to look for ancient coins and other objects. At that site everybody was looking for something. The picturesque figures, seen from far away, looked like a dance performance. People bending down and people getting up. The music was the Beer-Sheba wind.

Some of those old houses were built on the site of ancient tombs. Some people who lived there enlarged their homes with the very big caves that were underneath. The strange couple had a cave like that.

It is said that when they found that cave, a big coffin was found. Archaeologists who came to inspect the discovery said that it was from the Hellenistic–Roman period. Since the sarcophagus had no inscriptions or decorations, it was not very important. It stayed there and it was used by the strange couple to pile up the big bags they had all over the cave.

Archaeologists tried to find out if anything else had been found in the cave, but the old couple would not answer their questions. They never did. The archaeologists tried every language: Hebrew, Yiddish, Polish, Russian and Rumanian. In the end they gave up. No answer. The old couple laughed, showing the few teeth they still had in their mouths.

At the only window that still could be seen, was a glass pitcher. It had a single flower in it. When one of the group told the others to look at that phenomenon – a flower in a blue vase in the middle of all that dirt, bags and rubbish – everybody laughed. The old couple most of all.

One of the archaeologists said, pointing at the vase with the flower, 'It looks like a Sidonian glass pitcher.'

'Probably an imitation that they found in a trash can,' said someone else.

A few years later the old man died. The old lady continued to collect every day. She continued talking to her man, who was not with her any more.

After the rains I used to see her. She used to find some ancient coins or other metal pieces. I bought them all. For her it was the same if they were coins or Coca-Cola caps. I never bought a coin from her of value, or on which you could see something. But it was a *mitzvah*.

It was early evening when children came to call me. They said the old woman had found two silver coins. I was curious and went to see her. She was sitting on the bags next to the window. She was looking at the flower in the glass pitcher. When I came closer to the pitcher, I realized that it was an original Sidonian glass. It was the mould-blowing art from the first century.

It was an original Ennion. I thought that I was dreaming. The woman, the ancient pitcher and the flower. I held the piece in my hands and I saw the Greek inscription: 'Ennion made it'. It was exactly like the one in the Ha'aretz Museum in Tel-Aviv. I was sure now that this object and the one in our museum and the one in the Metropolitan were blown in the same moulds.

'Please hear what I have to say to you. You have here something that is worth a fortune. You can be rich. You can buy yourself an apartment, new furniture, everything, and still have money to live like a queen.'

She started laughing at me. She did not understand. She took the pitcher back and put the flower back.

Six months later there was a big fire. She was in hospital fighting for her life. Police and young volunteers helped to bring out what was left from the burned bags. It was the big discovery. Thousands of old money bills half burned, money that was not in use for over thirty years. Coins, jugs, pots, clothing. Everything gone with the fire. Next to the window was a mound of tiny blue-black burned glass chips, and next to that a burned flower.

They needed two trucks to carry away all the things that the old couple had collected throughout their lives. I think that the best piece they had in their collection was an original Ennion of Sidon pitcher – or was it just a vase for a flower?

Antiques and Toilet Paper

Zurich is the city for antiques and money. The beautiful shops and antique galleries are a tourist's paradise. Dealers from all over the world come to this Swiss city to do business. Many times I used to buy antiques in one gallery and sell them next door. Only a few local antique dealers visit their fellow competitors. They usually do business among themselves only through auctions, and then through a third person.

Dealing is completely different in Zurich and all other Swiss cities from Tel-Aviv and Jerusalem. Galleries in Zurich are like pharmacies. Every piece sits there: impeccable, clean and shiny. I love the pieces that are exhibited like kings. I do not care if there is a little dust here and there. I think it goes with it. It shows life. When an artifact comes into its new home, it gets a little dust too. I think that dust is the language of love for antiques, that is, when a piece is taken care of. It is like a baby, you hold it while you dust it.

When art objects are sold, they come in fancy boxes wrapped in bubble plastic. Arab dealers use toilet paper to wrap their antiquities.

I was holding a Greek vase that I had been offered, when an Arab antique dealer entered that gallery in Zurich. He was carrying a big suitcase, and with very bad English he introduced himself: 'You buy antiques? I am from Syria. Antique dealer from Syria.'

The Swiss dealer gave him a big smile, but at the same time looked rather cautious.

'Yes, we do buy antiques.'

The Arab antique dealer opened his suitcase on the floor and sat next to it. Inside were many objects packed in toilet paper. I was not surprised to see such a show, because in Israel we are used to seeing antiques wrapped in toilet paper.

While he was unwrapping the artifacts, toilet paper started to pile up next to the dealer and his suitcase. The gallery started to look a mess. The poor Swiss, who did not quite understand the whole situation, was almost in a panic. He was not looking at the antiquities, but what was all around them. He said to me, in German, 'Do you trust this man? I think that these are not real things.'

'Do you speak Arabic?' asked the visitor, addressing the Swiss dealer.

'Yes,' I answered.

'I have here a very large collection of glass and pottery.' The Syrian again sat on the floor next to his suitcase. The Swiss was sweating and was very nervous. He did not know what to do. Again he addressed me in German: 'I would like this man out of here. I really do not know what to do. Can you help me?'

'If you do not object, maybe I would like to buy from this dealer.' The Syrian dealer thought that we were commenting about the piece he was holding in his hand.

'Yes, very good piece. I make you special price.'

'Yes, you can buy whatever you want, but not here. Look what he is doing here. People will not enter this gallery when they see this mess. All this toilet paper lying around . . . '

'Here please' – I said in Arabic – 'Here is the address of my hotel. I shall see you in thirty minutes. Please pack all this up, and maybe we shall do some business.'

The Syrian dealer again started to wrap everything with his toilet paper. I was very excited, on the one hand, but very surprised, on the other, that the Swiss dealer did not even look at the antiquities that the man had.

I said goodbye to my host, telling him that I'd be back with the antiquities that I'd brought with me, but first I wanted to see what the Syrian dealer had to offer.

The Syrian dealer did not even have the chance to open all his little packages, and I was very glad that he had not opened them.

Thirty minutes later, in my hotel room, I felt as if I was at home. The suitcase on the floor. The toilet paper all around. The antiquities on the table, and the big discussion started. As usual the price was very high and I offered ten per cent of his asking price.

During my years of dealing with Arab dealers, I have learned that if you pay the asking price the seller will be very angry; not only that, but he will be very offended. It means that you are cheating him, and that the value is actually much higher than he asked for it in the first place. It means also that you'll never deal with him again. Bargain is the name of the game. The Arab dealer will swear to Allah (at least thirty times during the negotiation) either that it cost him much more, or that he is losing money, or that he is giving you all his merchandise only because he likes you. Many times he will say, take it without money, but what he means is that he is sticking to his price.

'If you buy it all, I'll make you a special price.'

'No, I am interested only in these five pieces.'

'These five pieces are the best ones in the whole collection.'

'Then keep them, I'll buy these four.'

'For these four I paid very expensive . . . '

'Then maybe I'll buy these others.' The game was clear to both of us. The man studied my reaction the same way I studied his. It was clear that he wanted to sell all, and it was also clear that I wanted the complete collection.

'If you buy all, I have a few other things at the airport, at the customs.'

'Why at the customs?'

'Because they are made of stone. Big stones. Jewish stones.' Now my interest became even bigger. To have Jewish archaeology was most important for me.

'I would like to see them.'

'After we finish this business.' The man had the feeling that he had me in his hands. I knew it also, but now it was my turn in this game of poker.

'This is my last offer to you.' I mentioned a sum.

'This is the lowest I can sell them to you.' He said how much he wanted. His first price and his last price were completely different.

'No thank you. It is too high.'

'Sorry, maybe next time. I paid much more for all of them. I swear on the light of my eyes.'

'Maybe you paid too much. No thank you. Maybe next time.'

The Syrian started to wrap again all the little perfume bottles and the pottery vases. He looked angry. Now we were at the height of our dealing – I had to let him pack, and let him leave. The big moment would come when he stepped out of the room: he would want a little more money than I had offered. In that case I would get the collection for my price. But if the dealer would not speak, then that would mean that he really had paid more, and that was my cue to increase my offer.

In the event, I bought the collection. I paid more. An hour later we were at the airport. I saw only one of the stones, which was decorated with the *menorah*. I did not want to see the others. I knew what they were. They were part of an ancient synagogue in Syria. I was sure of the period. It was Byzantine. I asked him for his price, showing almost no interest in the stones. He mentioned his price. I was the strong one now. He did not want to pay customs duty. I made my offer: 'That is all that I can pay for them. If not, send them back to Assad.' The Syrian accepted my offer.

That was my best purchase in years. It was not only a good business deal, but it was also saving ancient Jewish art and bringing it home. To Israel.

I knew where the pieces came from. It is perhaps twenty minutes' drive from Syria to Israel, but Zurich is a good place to deal.

It was already evening, and almost closing time, when I entered the Swiss dealer's gallery again.

'Did you do any business with the Syrian?'

'Just a little . . . '

'I am very sorry, but I am not used to it.'

'It is a different mentality; it is a different way of dealing. By the way, here I have brought you a few things that you might be intrested in.' I showed him a few pieces that I bought from the Syrian – the ones I was not interested in. After a short European discussion, the Swiss dealer paid for my whole purchase from the Syrian dealer. They were not wrapped in toilet paper.

The Fisherman

He was born in Tangier and owned a little fishing boat. He was a very short, thin man. He started his day at three o'clock in the morning. A small boy from nowhere was his fishing partner. He had an eternal cigarette in his mouth, and a metallic bottle in his pocket.

Whenever there was a fishermen's fight, he was involved. Every fisherman in Old Jaffa knew that he was not a very good fisherman. Even in very good times, when fish used to love fishermen so much that prices had to go down, he did not make enough for his living.

He had three places to live in; three women waited for him every night. Only one was the lucky one each time. There were also about fourteen children who looked like the very short fisherman.

He used to work for about two hours, when other fishermen used to work eight. The rest of the day he played dominoes in one of the little alleys of Jaffa next to the tower clock. He always sat at the same table, on the same chair.

He was called 'The Actor' by his fellow fishermen, because of his outfit. He always wore a black shirt, black trousers, black shoes and a black Greek fisherman's hat. On his little finger he had a gold ring. It was a very special one. It was an intaglio ring from the period of Caesar Traianus, from the year 98 CE. That ring was the envy of every person who saw it. Tourists used to offer him big sums of money for it, but the only thing they got, at best, was the story of the ring.

In the old days, he used to fish in Tangier and the south of Spain. He used to say that he knew where a Roman ship was, and that, when he found it, he would not have to fish for anything except antiquities. He was looking for a ship once belonging to the Romans in the sea in Jaffa. He said the day would come that he would find one.

Every time a fisherman found antiquities in his net it was a big occasion. Fishermen from all over the country came to see the finds. The stories behind these discoveries were even more important. As well as the stories, there was a good deal of fantasy that grew as the stories spread. All the fishermen knew exactly about every one of those finds. The only ones who did not know were the government officials. If the story came to their ears, it was always over five miles out to sea that the discovery was made. So, no bad feelings.

'The Actor' always waited for a windy and rainy day. Those were the days when fishermen used to stay home, whereas he was the only one that was on his boat, risking his life. He used to tell his friends that he knew the way that the waves had to be, in the sea, that in case there was a ship it would be flooded by the waves.

The actor–fisherman used to visit my gallery at least once a week. He was always interested in things that came out of the sea. I had heard the same stories, from Tangier and the south of Spain, several times. They used to change according to the fisherman's mood.

'You are going to be the first one to see what I found. I promise.'

'Tell me the story of your beautiful ring.'

'It happened many years ago. It was next to the seashore of Bolonia, the south of Spain. There is an ancient city that was built by Traianus the Caesar. As children, we used to cross the sea between North Africa and the south of Spain. We used to find antiquities that were lying there. When the foreigners came to excavate, we were hired. We stole whatever we could. One night there was a very big storm. We had to help to fix the tents that stood helpless in the wind. I looked at the seashore, and a very big jar came out from the sea. It was like the birth of a baby. It was all covered with shells. It was beautiful. Nobody saw that I took the big jar to a hiding place. What was more important than the big jar, for me, was the movement of the sea. I saw that something big moved in the depth of the sea. At that moment, I understood that a ship was there. I marked the place in my memory, for the future. I kept it a secret. When all the members of that archaeological team had left, and life was normal again, I sold the big jar to an American tourist, and with the money I bought a little fisherman's boat.'

'That is all very interesting, but you did not tell me about the ring.'

'Oh, I always forget, when I start talking. Yes, the ring. I went out to that place again. It had to be at night. A storm was coming from the east. I cast my net in the water and let it sink slowly. Not the way you do when you want to fish. I waited a long time for a wave under my boat. I knew it had to come, and it came. Then, very slowly, I started to pull. I felt I had something very heavy in my net. There were two jars with very big handles. They are called amphoras; and there was also a clay box. When I had them all in the boat, I opened the box that was sealed. It contained hundreds of little green coins, a pair of gold ear-rings and this ring. I was young and stupid; I sold everything, except this ring. I'll never sell it. Let archaeologists find my tomb with my ring and go crazy.'

Months later, he was sitting in my gallery again. He lit his cigarette with another, and pulled out from a plastic bag a little statue. It was Aphrodite. A beautiful bronze figurine.

'You see, I told you. I also told all my friends that some day I was going to find a Roman ship in the sea. This is the proof.'

'How did you find the ship?'

'For many years I knew that in a certain place was something. I do not know how to explain it. But I knew. I tried in very stormy weather with my net. Always the same place. Last night I was lucky. I saw the wave under my boat ... '

'Did you find any more things?'

'Here, look at this. A pottery plate. Look at all the seashells on it.'

'Do you want to sell your catch?'

'Yes. Make me an offer. But it has to be a really good one, because I waited so many years for these fish to bite.' He laughed, very loudly. He was very happy. I made an offer and he accepted. That was the beginning. He asked me not to tell anybody and I did not.

For months I saw the man playing dominoes outside the little coffee house in Old Jaffa. His friends said that he did not work any more. I knew that he was waiting for stormy weather. He was a fisherman who knew exactly which fish he wanted in his net.

Phases of the Moon

A group of young tourists from Toronto entered the gallery. They were young married couples on their honeymoons to the Holy Land.

I started to explain about the different archaeological periods. They were fascinated. Since they were young, I showed them inexpensive antiquities, in the hope that maybe some day they would be collectors.

He was young, blond, tall and very good-looking. He could have been a movie actor. His young wife was a very beautiful woman. Long black hair, green eyes. They were together what one could see in a fashion magazine. The perfect young couple.

During the time that these young couples were trying to decide on their first archaeological purchase, another group of young people entered the gallery. They came from New York. Among this group was a beautiful young girl. She walked on crutches. She started to hold an ancient oil lamp, and waited till I could attend to her. I was talking to the young blond fellow when he asked about an ancient oil lamp that he had seen before. When I approached the table where the oil lamps were, I started looking for it but could not find it. Then I heard her voice: 'Hello, how are you? Could you please tell me more about this oil lamp?'

'Good evening. Yes, you are holding an oil lamp from the period of the Maccabees. You see, the revolution of the Maccabees was not only what we know about it. The renewal of the

temple and the war against Hellenism. It was not only what we know about Hanukah and its miracle . . . '

'Excuse me, but I would like to hear it too,' said the young blond man, coming closer to the young lady with the crutches.

'Sure, why not. You see, at that time, the period of the Maccabees, closed types of oil lamps were in use. Most of them were made in moulds. Here, you can see a few of them from that period. The Maccabees, from the Hasmonean House, created a new type of oil lamp. What they actually did was to copy the oil lamp from the period of the Kings. I mean the type of oil lamp that looks like a shell. You can see that they were much bigger and more open.'

'This is extraordinary!' said the young girl, bringing one crutch from the left to the right, to hold the oil lamp from the period of the Kings in her hand.

'Please let me help you. I'll bring you a chair.' Before she could answer, the young man brought a chair, and she sat down. He took her crutches and laid them at her side. His young wife came over and was very impatient: 'Maybe you will choose your oil lamp now, or we'll come back some other day . . . '

I continued explaining: 'So what the Maccabees actually did was to make a modern type of oil lamp that was known eight hundred years ago. The same type of oil lamp, only much smaller, and at the end they pressed the sides of the oil lamp so that they would be closed. They did not want to use the oil lamps of the Greeks.'

'Julian, I think we must go. You see, our group has already left.'

'Please let the man finish.'

'This lamp, in the way it was done, was not very efficient. It is very simple. Not much air could come to the place where the wick lay, and the flame was very small. Archaeologists explain that this was actually the miracle of Hanukah. The little oil lamp burned much longer than any other from the same period.'

'Julian, please . . . '

'I think I would like to buy this one,' said the young lady with the crutches.

'I would like to buy it, too.'

'I have two oil lamps. Actually, they were found together, south of Jerusalem.'

'Could you please wrap the oil lamp my husband is buying first? We are in a hurry.'

'No, I think that this young lady should have hers first,' Julian said to his impatient wife.

'Your name, please?'

'Romia. Romia Levingstone.' I finished wrapping the oil lamp, and handed her the receipt and certificate.

'I'll be back again in April. Maybe I'll buy something else. It is my first antiquity. Thank you very much. Thank you too' – looking at Julian – 'You are very kind.'

'OK, now I'll have mine.' He smiled at her: 'You know, I am very happy that our oil lamps were found in the same place, and that we are buying them at the same place, at the same time.'

Romia smiled back, and let herself out, passing Julian's wife, who had to step to the side so that Romia could pass with her crutches.

It was already very late when I closed the gallery. While I was putting on the last lock, I raised my head and looked at the sky. The moon was there. The first quarter.

Months later, I recognized Julian. He was back. He was looking at the showcases. I was sitting in my office, and saw him through the mirror. He was alone. He went over to the place where the oil lamps were exhibited and started to examine them, one after another.

'Good evening, Julian. How are you? Nice to have you back.'

'I am happy to be back. This time I am not a tourist. I made *Aliyah*. I am an Israeli now.'

'I am very pleased to hear it. We need young people like you in the country. You can now help to build your own country.'

'Yes, I am learning Hebrew at the Ulpan. I have already been there for three weeks now. When I finish the Ulpan, I'll have to requalify at the university. I am a lawyer, and I want to work here as a lawyer too.'

'That sounds great, Julian. Welcome to your country.'

'I am divorced now.'

'I'm sorry.'

'Don't be. She did not want this kind of life anyway. Actually, we started to fight the day that I bought that Maccabean oil lamp.'

'I am really sorry, but . . . '

'Please don't be. It would have happened anyway.'

'But you were like a perfect couple, or . . . '

'Let's not talk about it. Tell me, please, did you ever see Romia again?'

'You mean the young lady on the crutches?'

'Yes.'

'No, she did not come back. Maybe she will. But I seem to remember that she said she'd be back in April.'

'It is now March. I really would like to buy something, but now I don't know what. Last time it was easy. Please, if you see her, please can you give her this card, with my address and phone number.'

'I can do that. You know what, I am going to put your card under my phone, so if I see her I'll have your address handy.'

After Julian left, I started to think about the girl with the crutches. The complete scene was before my eyes again. I started to close the gallery. It was night again. When I closed the door, I felt that I had to look at the sky again. It was the last quarter.

It was a Thursday evening. There were many people in the gallery when the phone rang:

'Good evening. Could you please tell me till what time are you open?'

'Till eleven thirty,' I answered impatiently. I did not like to be on the phone when I had people in the gallery.

'I am in Jerusalem. I would like to come to your place. I am leaving tomorrow. I want to buy something.'

'Who is speaking, please?'

'I don't think you'll remember me. I bought something from you. An ancient oil lamp. My name is Romia Levingstone.'

At first I did not recognize the name, but after a few seconds: 'Romia! I am so pleased to hear your voice. I'll wait for you. I really want to see you!'

It was eleven thirty when she came in. She came with her mother. She looked beautiful. She sat next to me, at my desk, and laid her crutches aside.

'When did you arrive?'

'Oh, we have spent some time here. In Jerusalem. I had an operation at the Hadassa hospital. I have a good chance of recovery. My right leg. It is much better now.'

'I am very happy to hear it.' I did not want to ask any questions, but she looked happy, and that was all that mattered to me.

'This time I would like to buy a lamp from the period of the Kings. So I'll have the two periods. Look, mother, how beautiful!'

While I was wrapping the ancient oil lamp, I told her that the good-looking young fellow from the last time was back, and had asked about her.

'Julian? How is he?' She had not forgotten the name, and her eyes were like very big stars.

'If you want to know, I have his address.' She said yes with her eyes. I understood. While I went to the phone, I told her Julian's story, in just a few words. I handed her the card.

It was twelve thirty. It was a beautiful night. There was a full moon. Somehow there had to be.

Julian and Romia came to the gallery a year later. She entered first, with her crutches; he came after her, pushing a baby carriage.

'We've brought you a new customer. His name is Yehudah, remember, the Maccabees? You'll have to explain to him all the periods.'

We burst into laughter. I knew it was evening and the moon was outside, waiting for me to put on the last lock. They were not a couple from the fashion magazine. They were part of one or, maybe, of all the phases of the moon.

The Ring

There are many little shops on Spiegelstratt in Amsterdam. Many antique shops. In past times, everyone could get genuine antiques. Today you can get genuine replicas.

The Wolf sisters were something of an institution in Amsterdam. They were originally from Germany. From Berlin. They were already old when I first met them. It is said that they were already old forty years ago.

The Wolf sisters had a beautiful collection of antiques, and especially of Judaica. Their sources were endless, for two reasons: first, because they brought with them a big collection of antiques; and second, because they lived in Holland. The place that protected Jews and gave them shelter for many centuries, ever since the Inquisition.

Every collector of Judaica dreams to have Jewish ceremonial art from the period of the Inquisition. Something that is almost impossible these days.

Antique Dutch Jewish ceremonial art was scarce many years ago, although there is one shop on the Spiegelstratt that by a miracle always had one piece. Today, collectors know that the owner makes them himself. But each time I am in Amsterdam, and see a new piece at the corner of the shop window, I know that the last collector did not know, and that the new piece is waiting for the next collector, who has to learn.

As I said, the Wolf sisters had a great collection. Their shop started to change when one of the sisters died. The younger sister

– if she was the one – continued to sell antiques, but it was not the same any more. When the second sister died, their collection was sold for a small fortune.

Twenty years ago, the sisters had a ring. It was something that I had never seen before, though it reminded me of an antique Jewish ceremonial wedding ring. The ring was very highly priced. The Wolf sisters were known for their modesty in prices. They were too modest to ask four or five times the value of the piece. With modesty, they asked only three times its value. They wanted to be sure that there was no loss – God forbid – on their sale.

Still, I loved to do business with the two sisters. We were friends, and that is maybe why I was invited, every time, for a cup of tea. Also their price was considerably lower, because of our friendship. The two sisters also bought from me, so there was always an open account.

One of the sisters told me that the antique ring was Jewish–Italian. The other was angry with her sister, because she thought that it was Jewish–Portuguese. I loved to hear their professional opinions and the way they disagreed.

The second time I saw the ring, it was said that it was Portu-guese–Italian; that was the day I knew the sisters agreed. I bought the ring. I was not sure if it was Italian or Portuguese; I was not even sure that it was Jewish. I was sure though that it was an antique, and at that time that was enough for me.

I showed the ring to every collector of Judaica I knew, until I did not show it any more. My collectors showed no interest in the ring, so this beautiful antique found its way into the showcase, for a long time to come.

He lived in Munich, had a very large collection of antiques and two Mercedes 600s. The first time he visited the Holy Land, with his family, I met him. So did every antique dealer in the country. Everybody was talking about the rich German who was looking for very special antiques, but nobody knew exactly what.

'What is this ring?'

'I do not know.'

'This is the first time in my life that I hear that a dealer does not know what he is selling.'

'It is true. I do not know.'

149

'So, if you don't know, what is the price?'

'I am not selling it, for now ... not until I know what it is.'

'This is incredible. You don't know, you don't sell?'

'There are so many antiques and antiquities in this gallery, is this the only thing that interests you?'

'Yes.'

The man left, very angry. Somehow I knew that next day I would be the talk of the town. I did not care. I still believe that when a dealer does not know what to say, he should simply say, 'I don't know.'

Two days later the German was back: 'OK, you can tell me the price now. I am alone – I suppose you didn't want to tell me the price while my wife was here.'

'The answer is still the same. I do not know anything about this antique ring, so I am not going to sell it.'

'I talked to dealers; they told me that you know very well what you sell.'

'I do, but this I do not. Is that so difficult to understand?'

'I propose a deal. I have Jewish objects in Germany that I bought, after the war, in open markets. Not because I am a collector of Jewish things, but because I liked the shapes and they were cheap. I am willing to exchange them for this ring.'

'It is a nice offer. Please send me pictures of what you have, and I shall consider your offer.'

The man went, and I was left with some question marks. The first was that I felt sure that the German knew what my ring was, and the second was that I did not believe that he had Jewish objects that belonged to Jews in Germany, and that he had bought them in markets after the war.

Two months later, I received his letter. It included photographs of Jewish ceremonial art objects; in particular there were three *ketubot*, marriage contracts.

I did not know what to do. My feelings were ambivalent. To give away a ring that I did not know what it was nor its value, or to get back the Jewish ceremonial objects, just because they were Jewish. There was another question to be answered also: what if the ring was Jewish?

I went to my rabbi for advice. I explained the case, and answered every question I was asked. It took a very long time.

'You should bring back the Jewish things which you know are Jewish, and if the ring turns out to be Jewish, so let it be ... '

I did as he said. It was the first time that I sold something I could not identify, but I knew what I got in return.

Queen Esther

Purim has been known for a very long time. Its history dates back to the time of the uprising of the Maccabees. Under the strong leadership of Nicanor, a powerful army was sent against Judas Maccabeus. Nicanor's army was defeated near Beth-Horon and Nicanor himself was killed on the battlefield. Nicanor's defeat created a lasting impression. In its honour, a special feast was dedicated: 'Nicanor's Day'.

Many years later, this festivity was unified with the oriental feast of the Sacae, which had nothing to do with the previous festivity. Their merging finally resulted in the feast of Purim, which we all know today.

The festivity is based on the Book of Esther – the Megillah – in which the elements of Persian–Babylonian mythology are preserved, even in the names of the protagonists: Esther, who is Ishtar; Mordechai, who is Marduk.

Esther is always the beautiful queen of Purim. She is always dressed in white, like a bride. Every year she comes back and brings loving smiles to the faces of the children of Israel.

Esther was her name. She was born in Prague, and when she was a little girl, her parents moved to Germany. They were a very wealthy family, and when Purim used to come, during the last rains of the winter, she was dressed in a most beautiful dress and a little silver woven crown.

When Esther's parents received the notice that her grandfather had died, the event changed their lives. Business was not good any more, and times were bad. Esther had to wear, at the coming Purim, the same dress of last year, which was altered to fit her.

Esther's mother knew how to sew very well, and little Esther looked beautiful. Nobody noticed that it was the old dress of last year.

The old grandfather left a will stating that he left some money to buy a *parochet* – a Torah shrine curtain – for the synagogue. Since the old man was born on Yom Kippur it had to be white, so it had to be hung only on the days of Rosh Hashanah and Yom Kippur.

As the times were bad and there was no money, Esther's parents used the money to live on. Esther's mother looked for all the old white dresses that Esther had worn, at Purim parties, since she was a little girl, and started to sew out of those dresses the curtain for the Torah shrine.

The little dresses had not enough material for the *parochet*, so Esther's mother used some other materials from the very nice dresses that she had worn in better times. There had to be, on the *parochet*, some writing – *Keter Torah* (crown of the Torah), and the name of the grandfather, to whom it was dedicated.

'I hope that grandfather in the sky – may his memory be blessed – will forgive us for not doing what he wished, in his will.'

'It is more important to live than to order, in these times, a new *parochet*, which costs a fortune.'

'He left the money for the *parochet*. All of it.'

'We are eating, we are living. That is more important.'

'I suppose so.'

'Do you think it is all right that we are making the *parochet* out of old Purim dresses?'

'Am I not going to be the queen next year? Am I not going to be Queen Esther?'

'You are always Queen Esther. You are always our queen.'

It is not known if that *parochet* was ever used in the synagogue. It was a beautiful *parochet*, with silver inscriptions that were a part of little Esther's silver-woven Purim crowns.

... The religious objects were taken into storage warehouses. Hundreds of scrolls of the law – the Torahs – lay side by side, like in a cemetery. Once they were the pride of the synagogues. These

Torahs were the lucky ones, they were not burned. Big bags containing *tallithim* (prayer shawls) and *tefillim* (phylacteries) were destroyed. They had belonged to dead men. They could not pray with them any more.

At that time, nobody knew about Bergen–Belsen, Terezin and Auschwitz. There, there were very big collections too. The macabre collection of shoes, teeth, glasses and hair . . .

The war was over. People started to smile. Many did not want to remember, many could not forget . . .

Esther was freed by the Americans. Like all the others in the concentration camp, she could not believe it was true. She was given a chocolate bar and ate it with the paper. She had eaten paper before. She was alive.

I met her many years ago. She used to come with her husband and children, once a year, to Israel. They lived in America. Esther and her husband had a very nice Judaica collection. She was always looking for a white *parochet*. That was the time I heard the story. Her story.

For many years after, whenever I saw a little girl as Queen Esther at Purim fesitivities, I remembered Esther's story. Somehow I always wished that I might be the one who could find the *parochet* that her mother had sewed from her little white dresses. Years later, I heard that in Berlin there was found, in a hidden place in a roof, a whole collection of *parochets*. Esther's was not there.

A very few beautiful and important ones are still exhibited these days. Maybe the most important one, now at the Jewish Museum in Berlin, is the one that was made in different periods. It was started at the beginning of the eighteenth century and then carefully added to, later on. A real work of art. When I first saw it I could visualize Esther's mother.

It was only a few years ago when Esther and her husband entered the gallery. She was very happy. After all those years of searching she had found her *parochet*:

'I was in an antique shop in New York. The owner knew my story and called me up. He was not sure if the *parochet* was the one I was looking for, but it was white and it was different from any other he had seen.'

'Did you get it?'

'Is that supposed to be a question, after all these years? Of course, but we have a story too. The *shamash* of the synagogue wanted to save two Torah scrolls, and he used the *parochet* to wrap them. He brought the scrolls to America with my *parochet*, would you believe that?'

'You know, I believe all the stories of the war. They are so incredible, and so true, that the biggest fantasy cannot create stories like that. Only the truth. Jewish history repeats itself. Haman wanted to kill all the Jews that were to be found in the one hundred and twenty provinces of the Persian Empire. Hitler wanted to kill all the Jews in the world. Maybe you are still the Queen Esther who, with her dresses, saved the two Torah scrolls, and the man carrying the Torahs was Mordechai. You see, Purim brings smiles to all the faces of the children of Israel.'

Angel Gabriel

Gabriel started to work as a carpenter. His father was one. Gabriel also liked to play cards. He thought that he was the best card-player, but had no luck. He used to lose all that he earned each day, and when games became more important than work there was less time for work and more for playing poker.

His luck, he said, was on vacation, but he was not; so he lost even more money than twelve carpenters could make. He had a good father, he said. His father had to sell his business to cover Gabriel's poker losses.

With tears in his eyes, and promising that he would never play again, he convinced his family, but not himself.

Gabriel's father had to work for another carpenter, at the flea market. Gabriel started to work as a helper in a shop. He became such a good card-player that the shop owner organized poker games in his shop, and was the man who put the money in Gabriel's hands. That was the time when Gabriel's luck was on duty, but Gabriel did not make much of it, because he played for his boss.

Mr Adam used to visit the flea market every day, and he liked Gabriel. Mr Adam had an antique shop and a very good heart. He loved to help people, and thought that he could even help Gabriel. He offered him a job at his shop with a chance to learn a profession. Gabriel was so happy that he had tears in his eyes. Had he been an actor, he would have received an academy award for his dramatic performance.

He worked for two years. Mr Adam explained how to recognize antiques and showed him the different books. Gabriel was present also when Mr Adam explained to his customers, and those were lessons too.

At the beginning, Gabriel really tried to listen, but when he started to come to work very late and tired, Mr Adam understood that Gabriel was more interested in other lessons. Poker lessons.

Gabriel told Mr Adam that he was not born for regular work. He wanted something big and he was going to get it. That was the day of the parting of the ways. Gabriel chose his own way and Mr Adam was not sorry. He knew that some day they were going to meet at another junction.

A few months later, Gabriel was the partner of an antique dealer at the flea market. He was on his own now. Once in a while, he visited his father, and the old man used to help his son in his new business. He always gave him what he had in his pockets. He was his only son.

Gabriel and Solomon were partners now, and their business flourished. No one in the flea market could compete with them. Gabriel and Solomon sold silverware, Judaica, objects of art. Their prices were so cheap that other dealers lost a lot of money in their businesses, because they bought their objects at a much higher price than Gabriel and Solomon sold their merchandise.

Mr Adam used to visit Gabriel's shop once in a while. He was worried about Gabriel's dealings. Something in Mr Adam's mind could not understand what was happening, and there had to be only one answer: they were selling stolen property.

Mr Adam knew that Gabriel was born with a natural high intelligence, and if something was going to happen it was Solomon who would have to pay for it. It happened. Gabriel and Solomon were arrested by the police. Gabriel was released and Solomon stayed.

'I have a special angel that takes care of me,' Gabriel used to say.

Mr Adam heard that Gabriel was taking care of Solomon's family while Solomon was in prison. Mr Adam understood that Gabriel was now a part of the underworld, because it was an underworld rule that if somebody took the blame for everything, and went to prison, the free man had to take care of everything else: money, cigarettes, whatever the man needed in prison, and his family at home.

'You know, Mr Adam, this country is too small for me. I have to enlarge my business. I am going to go international.'

Mr Adam did not want to talk to Gabriel any more, but he said, 'Good luck, Gabriel.'

Gabriel had many friends. They grew up in the same neighbourhood. It was funny, but Gabriel's friends were also the friends of the police. Once in a while they were arrested, for all kinds of crimes. But Gabriel always got away.

A few months later, there appeared on the market some very good pieces of Jewish ceremonial art. For some reason, they were always offered to religious antique dealers in Bnei-Brak. Only when those dealers did not buy did they come into other dealers' hands.

Gabriel had a car now. He came to visit Mr Adam. He told him that he was quite happy with the situation in the world. Mr Adam did not understand, and asked Gabriel what he meant.

'You see, we are now working internationally. We visit Communist countries, and we get Jewish things out of them. You see, I am very patriotic. The Communists do very bad things to Jews. They do not even let them out.'

'What do you mean by that?'

'Very simple. They exhibit Jewish objects, that were stolen from Jews, to show the world that they care about Jews and Judaism. That is good to show how socialism works. In culture, for them, everything Jewish has to be in a showcase.'

'Tell me more.'

'Is that so difficult to understand, Mr Adam? The Communists want Jewish pieces in showcases, and Jews in jails. We cannot open the jails where Jews are held, so we open the showcases.'

'This is terrible, Gabriel. You should not do things like that! You have a family and children, and a father.'

'I do not know much about morals. Jewish pieces should be in Jewish hands. I'll do that. And not only that, it gives me a good living.'

'Please leave, Gabriel. And do not come back any more.'

Mr Adam and I were sitting in the little coffee shop at Sheinkin Street. He told me the story.

'What do you think? Is that not a terrible thing?'

'In its way it is, but at the bottom of my heart there is something in that philosophy. Jewish objects in showcases and Jews in jails.'

'Not all Jews are in jail in Communist countries.'

'I wonder why they cannot leave those countries?'

38

The Way We See Things

The story, true or not, goes like this:

A worker from a factory, behind the Iron Curtain, used to leave the factory gates pushing a little wheelbarrow. The wheelbarrow was full of sand. Security officers checked that worker every day, and went through every grain of sand. They knew he was a *ganev* – a thief – but he never was caught. It was a very familiar scene. The worker, leaving the place daily after work, and pushing the wheelbarrow with the sand in it.

After months of searching this poor factory worker, the senior security officer decided to apologize and went to the worker's home. That day he discovered that the worker had over seventy wheelbarrows in his yard ...

It was an early morning. Soldiers and customs officers were standing at the Israeli side of the bridge. A truck started to cross the bridge slowly. When it arrived, it was stopped for inspection.

It was one of the open bridges between Israel and Jordan. It was the most brilliant step towards peace taken by one man. The open bridges policy. Moshe Dayan. These open bridges kept the real peace between Israel and Jordan, ever since the Six Day War. Maybe in politics things are different, but business conducts itself in its own way.

The truck was loaded with vegetables and fruit in heavy stone boxes. Small and big ones.

'I think that these people still live in the Stone Age.'

'I think that they never heard of modern packing and marketing,' answered the customs man, with a big laugh.

'Just imagine that they have to carry all those heavy stone boxes, without all those vegetables.'

'Should we tell them that these days we use cardboard boxes?'

The two customs men burst into laughter. Two hours later, in

Tel-Aviv, those primitive men with the truck were selling genuine antiquities, sarcophagi and ossuaries, to an antique dealer in Old Jaffa. They were not from the Stone Age, but artifacts at least two thousand years old.

The way we see things.

The bill that had been shown to the customs officers said: 'Original imitations of Roman sculpture'. They were two marble statues of early Roman gods. Apollo and Aphrodite. They weighed over two hundred kilograms each, and passed through the customs without any problem.

Two months later they were returned as 'unsatisfactory merchandise'

Now, the Italian government must be happy. Apollo and Aphrodite, which were strictly forbidden for export, were in Italy, and the collector in New York had two of the most beautiful authentic sculptures of Roman art.

The way we see things.

When the mummy of the famous Pharaoh, Rameses, left Egypt to be exhibited in Europe, the customs men had a problem of how to name that export according to the rules and the customs book. A solution was found: the mummy was stamped on the forehead with a stamp, according to the book: 'Dried Fish'. The ink stamps could not be removed, and poor Rameses never dreamed that after more than three thousand years he would be honoured with a new title: 'Dried Fish'.

The way we see things.

A very well-known Israeli physician visited Istambul. He was fascinated and fell in love with Istambul *shuck* – the market. He saw, he thought, an antique pistol. It was very cheap and he was very happy with his purchase. His happiness ended at the airport. He was arrested and the pistol was confiscated. The physician spent three months in jail until his case was heard. The man was accused of trying to smuggle out of Turkey 'a very important antique of Turkish history'. Israeli friends tried, in every way, to help the physician.

Two more months, and everything was solved. The physician paid a big fine. His name was in every paper. He was not very

162

lucky, but other tourists are. Hundreds of those pistols can be bought every day at the *shuck*. It is a Turkish tourist production. The 'antique' pistol factory works very hard to supply the demand. The physician still does not know why his pistol was so important. It was one of hundreds of pistols. He paid seventeen dollars for it.

The way we see things.

One morning, a German tourist entered the gallery. He was interested in an ancient coin of Alexander the Great. I showed him the coin and he fell in love with it. I told him the price and he fell out of love. 'I can buy thirty coins like that, in the old city of Jerusalem, for the price you are asking for one.'

'Go ahead. All the ways are open to Jerusalem.'

Two days later he was back. He showed his coin: 'Here, you see, I got it!'

I looked at his coin and did not answer.

'Is it real?'

'Do you want me to authenticate your coin? Do you need my expertise?'

'Yes.'

'This will cost you some money.'

'Can't you just tell me whether it was a good buy and if it is real?'

'If you want my expertise, you have to pay for it.'

The man left, furious. His face was red like a tomato. He did not even say goodbye. Three days later he was back.

'I heard about you. You are an expert. I want your opinion.' I told him the price again and started to write a receipt. I handed over the receipt and the man paid. Then, I started to write:

'This is a beautiful imitation of a coin of Alexander the Great. This is a cast from the Late Plastic period and is not older than a year or so. Real ancient coins and others are minted. This is not the case here. Therefore I hereby certify that this coin is a forgery, and has no numismatic value whatever.' I signed the paper and handed it to the man.

'You knew it from the beginning! Why did you not tell me?'

'If you go to a physician for a check-up and the physician tells you that you are healthy, do you not have to pay? Do you pay your doctor only if you are ill?' The man left, furious again. He mentioned a few words in German that were attributed to the weather, even though it was a very beautiful day.

The next day he was back. He bought the ancient coin of Alexander the Great.

The way we see things.

A Friend for Dinner

Collectors are very strange people. One thing all collectors have in common is that they are show-offs. First, every collector loves to introduce his antiques, as he would introduce his children. When a collection starts to grow, it has to be presented in showcases. When a collection is bigger, it needs a room. There are collectors who, when they need more space for their items, get rid of their wives and children.

Collectors may be divided into certain categories. There are the collectors of quantity and the collectors of quality. Collectors may also be classified as intellectuals and professionals. For the intellectuals, it is enough for them to know what they have, and in which book each item can be found, so they can show their collections with the proper intellectual background. The professionals want to be in the books, and if they succeed it is marked by wild enthusiasm. Collectors are also very good conversation partners – as long as they don't have to listen. They like to have complete attention and after that, like good actors, the applause.

He was always very friendly. He always knew how to make friends very fast. He always showed such loyalty to his friends that he was trusted.

He was a special friend of antique collectors, and tried very hard to help them to find new items for their collections. He used to go with them to shops, and when a collector found something he wanted for his collection, the friend always tried to help. He discussed the price with the owner of the shop and tried very hard to get the price down for the collector.

He used to be invited to almost every house, and collectors were very proud to show their friend their collections.

Collectors used to talk among themselves about this wonderful friend. How good he was, and how concerned he was to help. He was also unselfish and never seemed to want anything for himself.

He was also a dealer. He used to find things for his friends' collections, and always sold the antiques for the price that he bought them. He asked only a little sum above the price for expenses, and in many cases he used to get more money for the objects because of his kind-heartedness.

He was also a good friend of antique dealers, whom he used to visit almost every day. He always asked about the antiques, and his desire for knowledge was immense. He was especially interested in the rare pieces: their history, how much they were worth, and the best market for such objects.

He was invited for dinner. The collector told his friend about his last purchases, especially the ones that he got at bargain prices. He was also very proud of an antique which he had been looking for for a very long time.

'You will have to show it to me. This is all very exciting.'

'Wait, you have not seen everything. I have some pieces in my safe box.'

'I can't wait to see all those . . . Please could you pass the salt?'

'You see, with this object I started the collection . . . And with this one here my wife wanted a divorce when I told her the price I paid for it.'

'Was it so much?'

'Yes, but for this one I even paid much more.'

'You are a clever man. I am proud of you. These pieces do increase in value, don't they?'

'You see, this one here is worth twenty times the price I paid for it.'

'So it is actually the best investment.'

'You bet it is! My collection is worth now a few hundred thousand dollars.'

'Your insurance must be very expensive.'

'Actually I am under-insured. But nobody knows about these things. So I am not worried.'
'I have to thank you for showing me such a collection. It is like a museum. I am very proud to have a friend like you.'
'You are always very welcome. You will have to come again sometime for dinner.'

It was a very rainy night. It was winter. People went to bed early.
'You should close the window downstairs.'
'Yes, darling.' The man got up, and after a few minutes his wife heard him cry: 'We have been robbed! Everything is gone!'
The police were making a list of the stolen antiques. The man was calmer now. 'They stole only the most valuable pieces. Probably a special order.'
His antiques were not found. He told his story to his good friend at dinner. His friend almost cried when he heard the story. He had tears in his eyes: 'I am so sorry for you. Do you suspect anyone? Do you have enemies? Or maybe they were just lucky thieves.'
'Thank you for all you did for me. Especially for coming over to dinner.'
'You are my friend.'

Two months later, the friend was back for dinner.
'I think I have good news for you. I heard at the flea market that your collection can be bought back. I heard all that through a third person.'
'That is fantastic! Please help me, I am willing to pay everything to get it back!'
'Those thieves! They should be in jail! And now they even want money for what they stole.'
'Please try to make contact. I want my collection back. I'll pay you too.'
'Please don't offend me. I am your friend. You have to understand. I am taking a risk by contacting those men. So you understand – no police.'
'Of course not. I just want my collection back.'
Three days later the collection was back. All but one piece. The robbers were paid. The collector was very happy. He paid a very large amount of money, but he was happy.

'You have made me very happy. I am the happiest collector in the world now. Thank you, my friend.'

'It is only because I have very good contacts.'

'How much do I owe you, my friend?'

'I had some expenses. I paid two thousand dollars to my contact . . . that is all. I do not need anything for myself. We are friends, aren't we?'

'Here are the two thousand for your contact. And here are two thousand for you. You should get even more. This is just a token of our friendship.'

'You should not do this, but thank you.'

'I am the one who has to give thanks, Gabriel . . . '

The Expert

'A fool can throw a stone into the sea, and two hundred wise men cannot pull it out.'

It was just one of those days at Sheinkin Street. The tourist season was over, and the talking season had begun. Two o'clock on a Tel-Aviv afternoon. People and tables were outside. Stories were in the air and a few bottles of beer on the tables.

'Did you hear the story of Paul?'

'Which Paul?'

'The Frenchman, from the French Group.'

The French Group were antique dealers who spoke French, but actually they were all from Polish–Galicean families. They spoke French, and behaved as if they were the last generation of French noble families, before the French Revolution. These Polish–French lived in Paris before they came to Israel, and they all started at the flea market in Paris. They made enough money there so that in their new home country they could open very fancy antique shops, with French style and sophistication.

All the Polish–French were married to beautiful Moroccan women. Sometimes there were divorces, but the women stayed. They remarried another of the French Group. So it was not strange to see that when a little boy used to say 'Papa', another man from the group, and not the husband, would answer 'Yes'.

'Poor Paul had an original Galle lamp. A very beautiful lamp. A customer entered his shop and by accident knocked the lamp, which fell to the floor and broke into a thousand pieces.'

'The poor customer. What happened next?'

'Paul tried to calm his customer. He told him that he was insured, and that he only needed a statement saying what happened. The customer was so afraid that he would have to pay for it that he still was shaking when he had a cup of tea in his hand that Paul's wife had made him.'

'What is so unusual about breaking a piece that is insured? I think that the next round of beer is yours.'

'The next round is mine. Six beers, please! Well, Paul had his statement and called the insurance agent, who came very promptly. He saw the little pieces of the broken Galle lamp, wrote everything down, and told Paul not to worry.'

'Did Paul have to worry?'

'Only after Claude visited him.'

'You mean Claude of the French Group?'

'Yes.'

'What was there to worry about?'

'Claude came as the expert for the insurance company. Without even checking the broken pieces of the Galle lamp, he said, "This is not real. This is a fake."'

'Paul must have fainted.'

'He did. How can you say something like that to somebody? When he came round, Paul was furious. He said to Claude, "We were at the same auction in Paris when I bought this piece. You know it was real."'

'I'll buy this round of beer. It is starting to be interesting.'

'That lamp was worth at least fifteen thousand dollars. Paul was not a man who would give up easily. So when the insurance company said no to his claim, Paul was furious. It took him over three years in court to prove that his lamp was real. After three years, he got his money.'

'Why did Claude do that?'

'Claude is a person with a black heart. Whatever he has in his shop is real, even if it is a fake. Whatever somebody else has is always a fake. It is in his nature. There is nothing that can be done about it. Ever since then, Paul and Claude have not spoken to each other.

'Years later, there was a very nice collection of Galle vases in Claude's shop, in the show window. Behind those vases was a very beautiful Galle lamp. The lamp was decorated with a pattern of roses.'

'Don't tell us that the lamp resembled the lamp that Paul had.'

'It did resemble it. It was even the same size.'

'This is going to be funny. Go on.'

'My mouth is dry. I talk too much. Who is going to pay for the next round?'

'I will. What about some little sandwiches?'

'I'll pay for the sandwiches. You go on with the story.'

'Anyway, a very rich couple entered Claude's antique shop. An hour later they came out, with three Galle vases and the Galle lamp.'

'Poor couple! If they bought them from Claude they probably paid four times their value.'

'They did. Here, have a sandwich, they are good today.'

'The couple contacted the insurance company. They needed to insure the new purchases. They also wanted to make a revaluation of their collection. All that they had accumulated over the years was bought from Claude.'

'What did the man from the insurance company say?'

'The insurance man said that he wanted an expert to give an estimate of the value. That was when Paul came into the game.'

'Did Paul provide the expertise?'

'I think it is your turn. The table is weeping, and the bottles are empty.'

'Another round of beer, on my account please!'

'When Paul heard from the couple that the pieces were bought from Claude, he did not want to see the pieces, but he gave the name of an expert who was a real *meivin* – professional – of Galle.'

'I'll drink to that. That was a wonderful idea.'

'The expert came from Paris and after checking each piece he said: "All these pieces are fakes. All these pieces were made in some place in Europe, in the past few years, without a signature. The best way of knowing, before anything else, is by their weight. The fake Galle is much heavier than the genuine article. Now comes the most important thing. The signature. The signature was burned out with a special technique, with acids. So actually it is the same glass, nothing was added, and the signature is always burned out at the place where a flower was or a leaf was before, so it will not attract attention."'

'All the false Galle pieces were returned to Claude. He had to refund the money. His reputation, if he had one before, was nil.'

'So he knew that they were fakes.'

'Oh yes, he knew. I think that he also knew about Paul's lamp.'

'But was Paul's Galle lamp real?'

'The expert said yes.'

41

A Book from the Library

He belonged to one of the famous Jewish families. He had *yiches**.
He came from a very well-bred family. His great uncle had been a
famous rabbi who was very well-known in Europe. When the
family moved to Israel it was one of the most respected ones.

He came from that religious family, and was very intelligent
and well-educated.

My grandfather used to say, '*Yiches* may be inherited, but the
Torah you have to learn by yourself.'

He always looked like an English gentleman. His hand-tailored
suits were in the latest fashion. He knew the Torah and the
religious books, so that it was a pleasure to listen to this man. He
was a walking encyclopaedia. He was the one who in seconds
could tell the Hebrew date, comparing it with the Gregorian.
Others had to sit down and make the calculations.

The family of the great rabbi, his uncle, was a very rich one.
They had their own synagogue, and religious objects were given
as presents by the members. Personal gifts of Jewish ceremonial
art were the family's treasure.

He was married to a very fine woman who came from a *yiches*
home, too. Not only *yiches*, but money as well. He knew how to
spend it. He knew what and where to buy for himself. He was
very talented, and very capable in almost everything.

---

* Came from a noble and respected family.

Scholars and professors were among his friends, and they loved his company and shared his knowledge.

I first met him on Sheinkin Street. He came to one of the dealers to sell a very beautiful Jewish ceremonial Torah crown. It belonged to his family in Vienna. The piece was bought immediately, for two very good reasons: it was a good piece and it had *yiches*, that is, it came from one of the best-known families, and therefore its value was assured.

From time to time, Jewish ceremonial objects from that particular *yiches* were sold, and resold each time for much higher prices. There was always a very good market for those objects, even in the times when business was slow.

He was also a lawyer, and was always giving legal advice to people who needed it, but he really never worked at his profession. People always wondered how this gentleman made his living. Always very well-dressed, and even in the hot days, in the summer in Israel, he wore a three-piece suit.

He used to travel to England and the United States, and was very well-known there, too.

His reputation and *yiches* were international, and he knew it. He used to sit for hours in the university library, and when his friends, the professors, saw that he was working very hard, on Jewish subjects, they remarked, 'You are working very hard, Mordechai.'

'I have no choice. The books that I need are here.'

'It could be arranged . . . ' The professor signed for the books that Mordechai needed. They were very rare books, and some were unique.

'I do not know how to thank you. I'll bring them back as soon as I finish my work.'

'Take your time, there is no rush.'

More pieces of Jewish ceremonial art appeared on the Judaica market. These had belonged to the famous rabbi, Mordechai's great uncle. Some of the collectors used to go to that family's synagogue to see if anything there was missing. Nothing was. People knew that Mordechai's family had a large private collection and it seemed that everything was OK.

There were even times when a few Torah crowns were sold. Nobody suspected that anything was wrong. The problem began when Russian objects of Jewish art were supposed to be from the rabbi's court. As long as they were from Vienna, the place where the rabbi came from, people did not ask; but when the Russian pieces appeared, questions were asked. Mordechai was so convincing when he said that the old rabbi had Russian Jewish friends in that period, who presented gifts, that the explanation was accepted.

Very few people knew what was in the old rabbi's collection. When one of those who knew was approached, and asked if that piece really belonged to the old rabbi, he did not remember, but he gave the name of a man who had a very good memory.

That man remembered. He knew exactly about all the Jewish ceremonial pieces that had belonged to the family. When he saw the piece that he was shown, to identify, he was sure. He had never seen the piece before in his life.

Mordechai was asked to refund the money. Mordechai, who was very gifted in talking, tried to convince the man that he, Mordechai, and nobody else, knew best about the family's collection.

I was named the arbiter, by mutual agreement. I had the piece before me and there was no doubt that it was an authentic Russian Torah crown. It had sold for a very high price because of its *yiches*. I heard what Mordechai had to say, and heard as well the customer's complaint. I did not know what to say. I started to look at the Russian silver marks and asked a very simple question:

'When did the old rabbi, may his memory be blessed, die?' (That was not a secret. The date was very well-known).

'The late rabbi, may his memory be blessed, could not have received this crown. He was already dead, twenty years before this crown was made.'

A few months later it was in the paper that Mordechai, the gentleman, was to be on trial. He was charged with stealing very famous and rare books from the library of the university.

His system was a very simple one. He used to keep the rare books and return to the library the modern copies. At the beginning, nobody noticed that anything was missing. The books were there. It was recorded that the books had been returned. The poor professors were in trouble. They were the ones who had signed for the books. Mordechai almost convinced the court that, in many cases, the books that he had taken were the ones that he returned. In many cases it was very difficult to prove the contrary. He also promised to return the real books, but he did not.

Mordechai was found guilty and sent to prison, but not for long. He convinced whoever had to be convinced that he came from a very good family. He had *yiches*. After a few months, when Mordechai was asked what had happened, he put on a puzzled face which suggested he did not really understand what had happened: 'I was in London. I was very busy. I was writing a book . . . '

He continued to sell the 'rabbi's' collection for a long time. He was seen all over the world, in his hand-tailored English suits. When he explained some things about Judaism or Jewish ceremonial art, he knew what he was talking about.

One day Mordechai died. He was still young. Members of the old rabbi's synagogue said that once the old rabbi had called Mordechai to him, saying: '*Yiches* you have inherited, but what you need is a Torah lesson.'

Philosophy of Collecting

A collector is a person who adds one piece to the first he has. These two pieces are a collection. I believe that every person in this world is a collector. Everyone collects something, whether consciously or not.

I never met a person who has not a place where he keeps things, either for sentimental reasons, or because he does not want to get rid of them. Because he is simply attached to the objects. To be attached to objects is to collect them. In a day, or a week, you are going to be attached to another one, a new item of the collection. That is the second reason, and it is as sentimental as the first. Something that cannot be explained.

When did this all start? It was with pre-historic man. In his caves was found a collection of animal teeth that were lying there. He collected the teeth, made a hole in each one, and the first piece of jewellery was invented. A collection of teeth.

The archaeologists who found the teeth collected them, and they are now in the museum's collection.

In wars, the victorious army collected the weapons and religious objects of the defeated enemy and brought them home to show them to their people. Since there were no museums at those times, the show was in the centre of the town.

When the children of Israel left Egypt, it is said that they left with treasures. They did not bring gold coins or dollars – they were not available at that time – but sculptures, scarabs, idols, vases, urns, etc. That is why so many Egyptian archaeological objects are found in Israel. The children of Israel collected whatever was available in Egypt at that time.

Since there is no archaeological proof that newspapers existed in Roman times, the news of the collection that Roman soldiers brought from Jerusalem, after the destruction of the temple, was recorded at Titus Gate. That is the gate on which can be clearly

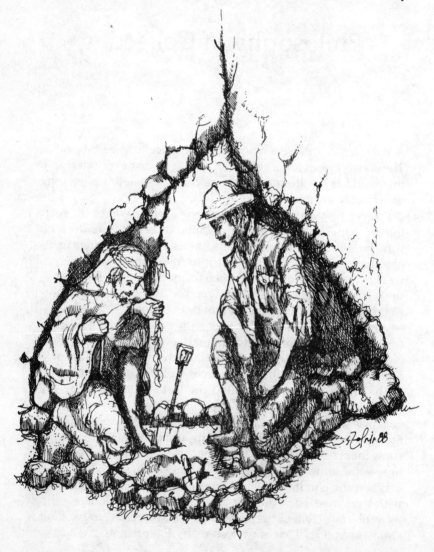

seen the catalogue of the collection that the Romans brought with them of Jewish ceremonial art. A very nice collection. All authentic from the Second Temple period.

But the disease of collecting is not confined to individuals. Big institutions, like the biggest in the world – the Church – love to collect. People, in the name of the Catholic Church, looted treasures from all over the world, the old world and the new, thus the 'fabulous collection of the Vatican treasures' was created.

The British Empire, in the name of its monarchy, stole antiques from all the places where the English spent some time, for one reason or another. That is known as 'the wonderful collection of ancient art at the British Museum'.

It is said that we Jews invented *chutzpah*, but I have some doubt as to who uses it best. When you see the looted archaeological objects at the British Museum, from Egypt, Greece, Israel, etc., they have little signs in front of every piece: 'In appreciation'. Of whom? Of the idiots who let their treasures be robbed?

When Melina Mercouri wanted the Greek pieces back for Greece, she was offered, very kindly, 'authentic replicas'. Is that not beautiful? How do the Greeks dare to try to destroy a collection that so much love was put into? This I call *chutzpah*!

If the man who planned the British Museum had bigger ideas at that time, they could have put all Old Athens in the Greek department at the British Museum. What a pity. All the Greek antiques would have been together.

The big fish eats the smaller ones, and so on. The same rule applies to collectors.

One of the finest collections in the world is the Rothschilds'. They collected the best that money could buy. The very first Rothschild, the old grandpapa, was an ancient coin collector who made his fortune by selling antique coins to the prince. The prince collected coins. The Rothschilds changed their hobby to collecting money, and when they had it they returned to their first love – collecting antiques.

All the millionaires of the world are art and antique collectors. I wonder why. But everybody is a collector, even the ones who look for things in dustbins. Children start to collect when they are very little. Poor children collect things from the streets and rich children get them from their parents. Collectables – not only the things they want. It is what their parents could not collect as children. These days, the production of children's collectables is a multi-million dollar enterprise. There are factories all over the world. Disneyland sells fantasy collectables. Millions buy them. Once, girls used to have one or two dolls in their toy collection. Today they have to have at least thirty Barbies. They all look the same, but they are collected.

Stickers are such a big business that factories pay fortunes for new names or ideas in stickers. They run out of names, not out of collectors.

Only thirty years ago, when children used to collect stamps, they would try very hard to get old envelopes from their families and friends. Now, these days, they try very hard to get the money to purchase them. Old stamps are not interesting enough for children. Today it is sports, flowers, boats and everything else. It has to be an unused stamp. There are countries whose income is based on the production of stamps.

Countries are collecting atomic bombs. Yes, collecting is the word for it. There are over three thousand atomic bombs in the world, while only fifty are needed to blow up our planet. It is like children who compete, who has a bigger collection. The same thing with atomic bomb collections.

There is not one single item in the world that is not collected. If an item does not exist, then it is created, the very next morning, to be collected.

Collections of the most naive things stand against the most barbarian and macabre collections, like the one of the Nazis.

Man was born as a collector.

When a child is born, he holds his hands as if he is trying to catch whatever he can get. The new collector is born. When a person dies, it is with open hands. He has finished collecting, and is not taking anything with him.

I wonder what is collected in heaven. I would dearly love to be an antique dealer there.

The Astarte Figurine

There are collectors who love antiques, and sometimes there are those who believe in them.

He was originally from Turkey. From the north. He was married and was a taxi driver.

'I heard that there are antique figurines that represent goddesses of fertility, is that true?'

'Yes. These figurines are called Astartes and they were goddesses of fertility.'

'If you have the time, could you tell me more about it? This subject is very interesting and I think I would like to collect them.'

'This figurine you see here is Anatolian. The Anatolian figurines were associated with fertility and birth. These female figurines were magical talismans supposed to ease the labour of childbirth and to increase fertility.'

'People believed that they worked, did they?'

'Absolutely. That was a tradition that existed thousands of years.'

'Do you think it might work these days? Oh, don't answer, I'm only joking!'

'People do believe in ancient superstitions.'

'I think I am going to buy this figurine.'

'Do you collect antiquities? You have never been here before?'

'No, I do not collect. Actually this is my first one. I am just interested in the subject.'

I was puzzled about my new customer. He was not the intellectual type of collector who collects ancient objects because the subject interests him. He was not a collector at all. It was for me a perplexing question, an enigma, of what this man would do with an ancient figurine of Astarte.

A year later he was back.

'I bought a book about Astartes, and I even went to the museum to see the Astarte collection. I think I would love to purchase an Israelite Astarte.'

'You know, there are actually no Israelite Astartes. You know that the Israelites have no gods or idols. You know what is the Second Commandment: "Thou shalt have no other gods before me." But in the Israelite period the Canaanites had a great influence, and because of that it is said that Israelite women had pottery figurines of Astarte in their homes, for fertility.'

'Of course! You don't have to tell me all that. I know. I am Jewish. It was just a matter of interest in the subject.'

'Here, you can see, I have two figurines that were found in Hebron.'

'I think I am going to buy this one. I like it more, because it has bigger breasts.'

'She is very sexy.'

'Do you think that Rachel from the Bible was hiding from her father Astartes like this one?'

'No, in the Bible it does not say there were Astartes. It says they were "*Teraphim*". Anyhow, nobody knows exactly what *Teraphim* are. The most important point is that the Torah was not given then to the children of Israel. That is why not all the *mitzvahs* that are in the Torah were observed at that time.'

'But this figurine is from the period of the Kings, isn't it?'

'Yes.'

'I am going to buy it.'

After the man left, the enigma was bigger. The big question I had to answer was, what did this man have in his mind? Why was this man buying Astartes? He was not interested in the archaeology of the pieces. He was interested in the function of the Astartes. The function of the magic, or any other power that those goddess figurines were supposed to have.

Months later, he was back. I think it was about ten months ago that the man last visited the gallery.

'I bought more books about the subject. I also went to see a professor of archaeology and he told me that Isis, the Egyptian goddess, was the real goddess of fertility.'

'What do you mean by "real"?'

'I mean that in ancient Egypt people did believe that Isis was the goddess of fertility, and people who had these figurines had children.'

'Maybe, but it does not say that people who did not have these figurines did not have children.'

'Exactly. These figurines were for people who could not have children.'

'The story of Isis is a very simple one. Isis was the sister and the wife of Osiris. She is shown in the figurines, like this one, seated on a throne. Isis wears her usual crown of cow's horns surrounding the sun disc. She is holding little Horus, who is her and Osiris's son.'

'If it were not a fertility figurine, she would not be holding Horus.'

'In a way, you are right.'

'I think that Isis is coming with me.'

When the man left, I began to wonder if maybe he had a personal problem. Something that had to do with fetishism. Something that attracted him so much to Astartes, the goddesses of fertility. It was also quite an expensive hobby for a taxi driver. Astartes are very dear. Nine months later he was back.

'I think that I would like to collect amulets. I saw that you have many. I wonder if I can exchange the Astartes I bought from you for a collection of amulets.'

'Sure you can. What made you change your mind from collecting Astartes?'

'I cannot tell you now. Maybe some other day. If you have some time, I would like you to tell me what you know about amulets.'

'Amulets started when special events in the family began, with the birth of the first child. The mystery that surrounded pregnancy, and superstitions and fantasy invented fears. Fears of unknown forces when a woman was waiting for her child to be born. Amulets were created, based on religion and mysticism. In some Jewish communities, people recited nine verses of the psalms, for the nine months of pregnancy. In others, special little plaques, like those you see here, had also verses of psalms and the writings of the names of the demons. These demons are called Sanoi and Sansanoi. There are also writings of the very special angel, who is called Samenglof. All these are to contribute to the welfare of the women in childbirth.'

'Please go on. How do you know all this? Do you have books about it?'

'It is kabalistic. It is all written in the holy books, but during all my years as an antique dealer I learned most of what I know from people I met. People from all communities of Israel.'

'Please go on. Tell me more.'

'In every Jewish community there are different traditions, and these vary also from family to family. In the Talmudic era, a woman who was pregnant received an amulet, on which the inscriptions were written especially for her and for her unborn child. When she gave birth, she was considered ill for thirty days; that was the time when she received special treatment.'

'This is wonderful.'

'You see in this amulet, that was made for the mother and infant, the image of the demon, Lilith, and around it is the Hebrew inscription: "Tear the devil" – which words actually come from the *shabbat* prayer. Each letter is the beginning of a word in the prayer, and when they are put together the words "Tear the devil" are formed.'

We made the exchange. The Astarte figurines for fertility were back. The man had now a collection of fertility amulets.

Almost a year had passed again. The man was back.

'I do not know what to do. I do not want to be a collector. I never had the intention to be one. I just wanted a child. I tried everything. My wife and I went to every doctor who we heard could help. They could not help. Every time my wife was pregnant, I did not let her do anything. We just want the baby. After two or three months, she loses it. Once even in the fifth month. I tried everything. Do not laugh. That is why I bought the Astartes; I would have bought anything. That is why I also bought the amulets. Nothing helped. Five times my wife lost her baby.'

'You have tried everything. Medicine, mystics, superstitions, legends, magic and archaeology. I think you should talk with my rabbi. You don't have to pay anything, and you certainly won't lose anything.'

That same day, we met at my rabbi's home. He told the man to bring all the *mezuzahs* he had in his home. He did that and was back with the parchments. My rabbi checked them, one by one, for a long time, and said to the man:

'You have to put new *mezuzahs* on your doorposts.'

The next day, a new *mezuzah* was on every door entrance. Ten months later, the taxi driver invited me for the *brithmilah*. The circumcision. It was a very happy occasion. I was the *sandak* – the godfather.

It was *shabbat* in the synagogue. The rabbi was speaking about the *mezuzah*:

'It has to be checked at least once a year. One letter or even part of a letter which is *passul* – meaning void – can change many things at home. One little *passul*, and the *mezuzah* is not kosher, and therefore cannot be used any more. It has to be buried.'

At the end of the ceremony, I approached the rabbi and asked what was wrong with the man's *mezuzahs*.

'There was a *passul* on one of the letters of the words: "Your children".'

44

The Last Piece of Silver

It was a sad evening. They were all there except the father. The mother had just told her children that she had sold the last piece of silverware they possessed. The money was for the family's needs, and with luck it would bring food for another three weeks.

It was the last piece of silverware she had received from her family for her wedding. That was thirteen years ago.

A wedding like that, people said, was not seen in years. There were over three hundred guests. Her rich father had provided for everything. He bought whatever was needed for the new couple. The quantity of objects he bought would have been sufficient for two couples. He wanted his daughter to feel comfortable, the same way she had felt when she was at her parents' home.

She did not know to whom to sell the silverware. The only person who used to buy art and religious objects was a man at the new immigrants' camp. He was the cook's helper.

He used to buy objects of art and jewellery for next to nothing. People who sold those objects only wanted to eat and live.

A few years later, the cook's helper bought a house in the centre of Tel-Aviv and opened an antique shop. Times were good for him, and he opened a second shop. Books figured prominently among the objects he bought. He was no intellectual. Books were so cheap that, in many cases, whenever he bought an object he made the people who were selling it throw in the books they had as part of the deal. That was how he accumulated his immense collection of books. People who were interested in books had to pay the highest prices for them, because at that time there were not many bookshops in Tel-Aviv.

The silverware that he bought from that woman was not for sale. He took every piece to his apartment, which was located on the second floor above his antique shop.

He was a very greedy man, so greedy that if a poor man ever

asked for a coin he was chased away. Charity was not one of his
virtues.

Moses was the first-born, and in Israel he was called Moshe.
When he was little he promised his mother: 'One day I am going
to earn a lot of money, and buy all the silverware back. I am going
to find every piece, and bring it to you, mama.'

'How are you going to know which are the ones that belonged
to us?' asked his little sister.

'I'll remember. I remember now. I still can see, before my eyes,
every piece.'

'Even if you don't remember, my son, there is a little mark on
every piece. It is so little that it can hardly be seen with the naked
eye. Your grandfather engraved his initials, using a magnifying
glass, and that marking is always in a place where the silver object
is most ornated, so it will not attract attention. In this book, you
can see the way he wrote his initials.'

The new antique dealer, who did not want to remember the days
when he was the cook's helper, was so greedy that he even had
problems with his four children. They had to sleep in one room,
all four of them, while in the other rooms were stored the antiques, the books and all the objects which he accumulated.

He never bought new clothing for his children. At first, when
he still was the cook's helper in the immigration camp, he asked
people for clothing. Later, when he was already an antique
dealer, he used to buy for his children old clothing that was sold
at the flea market.

His children hated him, but there was nothing they could do.
He was the one who fed them. In the years to come, his children
entered the antique business. But after a short time they did not
want to work for their father any more. Each one became an
antique dealer on his own.

Instead of working together and collaborating, they were enemies and the competition between father and children was the
biggest ever seen.

When they parted, each of his children demanded his share of
the antiques. That was the time when the old man had to part
with four silverware pieces he had bought from the woman in the
immigration camp. Now, each of his children had a silver piece

that the old man never wanted to part with. That made him even more furious.

That situation was sometimes very convenient for other antique dealers. They used to enter one of the shops of that family, and if the price was not reasonable they would say that they were going to find something similar, either at one of the brothers' shops or at the father's shop. The price went down. Sometimes the brothers were prepared to lose money on the deal, so as not to let the customer go to another brother's or to the father's shop.

Some years later, the old man had troubles. He had done something that he was not supposed to do. It was against the law, and he needed a good lawyer.

'You have to help me. I am in trouble.'

'You are not in trouble. You are in big trouble.'

'You have to help me. I am an old man, and I do not have many more years to live.'

'This is a very long case, and I will have to put a lot of work into it. It will cost you a lot of money.'

'How much?'

'The complete collection of silverware that I saw at your apartment.'

'It is not complete any more. I had to give four pieces to my children when we split up the business. So I can only give you what I have. All the silverware, except for the four pieces.'

'I am sorry, I am not going to take your case. Maybe you should forget about the silverware and pay me. This is my price.'

'So much?'

'Maybe you should go to another lawyer. Maybe somebody will take your case and handle it for less.'

The old man was furious: 'To pay such an amount of money! These lawyers must be daylight robbers.' He thought that he would be better off if he could get the four silverware pieces from his sons. All the other pieces he had cost him almost nothing. He went to the first one, who did not even want to speak to his father, but after a while the old man said that he wanted to buy the silver vase that the son had. The son demanded a price that was very, very high, but nevertheless the old man paid.

With two other sons it was the same story. For the first time in his life the old man paid the asking price. He was ashamed of himself, not only because of the large sums of money he had to pay his sons for the pieces, but because of the humiliation of it all.

The fourth son, who always was like the old man himself, was even worse. He first demanded an apology for all that the man had done. That was terrible. But the old man did apologize. Later on he left his son's home with the big silver plate. Now he had the whole collection. He put everything in a box; and somehow it reminded him of the days in the immigration camp, when he was the cook's helper.

'I've brought you the complete collection. You are very lucky that I have kept it during all these years.'

'OK, I'll take your case.'

Moses went round to his mother's house. He put the box containing the familiar pieces of silver on the table.

'The case was solved the way I wanted, Mother.'

She looked at the silver, then she looked at her son: 'You are a very good lawyer, Moses.'

The *Shamash*

The *shamash* – the useful one – is actually the ninth candle-holder for the Hanukah lamp. This is the one which has been used, for over two hundred years, to light the Hanukah candles. Its use to light the Hanukah candles comes from the bad translation of the Hebrew word *shamash*. Instead of 'the useful one', it was translated as 'the servant'. Hence its new use.

According to the Jewish law, Hanukah, which means the Feast of Dedication, is an eight-day festivity. This festivity began when the temple was purified by the Maccabees after it had been profaned by Antiochus Epiphanes and his men. The festival of Hanukah, which begins on the twenty-fifth day of *Kislev* (December), is one of the brightest holidays of the Jewish year.

Since the Hanukah lights, that are lit one more each day until the eighth day, are holy, and cannot be used in any way other than to look at them, the ninth light is the one which is used for lighting. That means that actually the one whose light is used is the *shamash* – the useful one.

There is also another *shamash* – a useful one – and that is the *shamash* of the synagogue, who is not the servant of the synagogue members, but the useful one in the synagogue.

The air raid, that day, was terrible. The bombs that came from the sky were endless. They were sitting in the shelter. The good women were distributing hot soup.

When the siren sounded the 'all clear', the mother told her son:
'You stay here. I just want to get some food.'

'Please hurry, Mother, the next bombing must be very soon
again.'

'Hold this, my son, and keep it.' The woman handed her son a
little wooden box. The little boy put the box in his pocket. The
mother addressed a woman who was sitting next to her: 'Could
you please watch my son for a while?'

'You won't be long?'

'I shouldn't think so. I just need to get some food.'

'It would be better if you stayed here. It's dangerous on the
streets now.'

'I'll be all right. Take care of my boy, will you please?'

'Sure.'

'God bless you.'

She did not return. The little boy stayed with the woman at the
shelter for a long time. The bombs fell all night.

'Your mother is probably in another shelter. She'll be back after
the air raid is over.'

'Yes, madam.'

'My name is Marion. Call me Marion.'

'Yes, Marion.'

Marion returned every day with the boy to the very same
shelter to find the boy's mother. After a month she gave up hope.
The boy was like a son to her, and she got used to the idea that she
had a son now.

The first time she washed the boy, she noticed that he was
circumcised. She said to herself, 'He is Jewish.' She did not care.
The boy was blond like her; he also had blue eyes. 'The way he
looks is all right. He will not attract attention.'

She was poor and worked in every way she could.

At first she took the little boy with her to church, but after a
while she thought that something that she was doing was wrong,
though she had all the rights to do so. She was the boy's mother
now. The only thing she did was to change the boy's name. She
called him Hans Dieter. He was brought up with that name.

He went to school with all the other children. One day, in the
afternoon, he asked Marion, 'Are Jews really that bad?'

She was shocked at the question. She started to think fast.
What should she say to the boy, who was now eleven years old?

'Jews are people like we are. There are good ones and there are bad ones. The same in any country in the whole world. There are good and bad people.'

'But children said . . . '

'Never mind what they say. You only listen to what I have to say.'

'Why is it that I do not have a father?'

'There are many things that you don't know yet. When you will be older, you are going to know everything. Maybe then I am going to know better myself too.'

He had the little wooden box in his room. The little box his mother gave him some years ago in the shelter. He opened the box many times, but he did not quite understand the two items that were inside. They were a little silver cup with a hook attached to it, and a piece of paper. The paper had a number and an address in Basel.

Many times, he and Marion used to sit and play with the little silver cup, and many times he asked Marion the meaning of the little hook that was attached to it. The number on the piece of paper and the address that was written below were also a puzzle.

Marion decided to go to the rabbi at the Jewish community centre. She told the story with simplicity. She told him that the real name of the boy was Isaac, and that she called him Hans Dieter. She told the rabbi about the boy's mother and what she looked like. She did not know her name. The boy was going to be thirteen years old, and she knew that the Jews had some festivity at that age. She asked the rabbi if she, as a non-Jewish woman, could help her son for the festivity, and what was she supposed to do.

'Your son has to learn the Torah, like any other Jewish boy of his age.'

'I would like that. When should he start?'

'First of all, I have to know that he is Jewish.'

'He is circumcised.'

'Is there something else that you know about his family?'

'His mother handed to him a little wooden box at the bomb shelter. I do not think it is very important. It is a little silver cup with a hook. Something very funny. I never saw a silver cup with a hook. There is also a note. A very strange note. It has a number of six digits, and below an address in a Swiss city, Basel.'

193

'I would like to see those things.'

'I'll bring them in tomorrow.'

That night Marion told her son the story. She told him that he was Jewish and that she went to the rabbi for his *barmitzvah*. She also told him that the rabbi wanted to see the box and the two things that were in it.

'I'll come with you, Marion. I do not want to part with the box or the cup or the paper.'

'You won't have to.'

'This is a *shamash*,' said the Rabbi. 'This is the useful one. This is part of a very old Hanukah lamp. The little hook was made so that this little cup, the *shamash*, could be attached to the Hanukah lamp.'

Marion and the boy did not understand. The old rabbi brought out his Hanukah lamp to show them. They were delighted and laughed. It was a happy occasion. The only enigma was the paper with the number and the address in Basel.

'That is not very difficult to find out. I mean the address. I shall call a friend I have there, and we'll know.'

'When do you think you can do it?' asked Marion.

'Right now.'

The old rabbi picked up the phone and started dialling. He talked to his friend for a few minutes and asked him what that address could be. The friend answered that he was going to find out, and was going to phone back the next day.

'The address you gave me is that of a Swiss bank. It was the same bank before the war too. The number you have is probably the number of a safe box in the bank.'

Three weeks later Marion and the boy were in Basel. It was true. In the safe box was a silver Hanukah lamp, without its *shamash*. There were also eighteen gold coins.

That year Marion's son had his *barmitzvah*. That was also the first year that Marion's son lit, for the first time in his life, his Hanukah lamp, with the little *shamash* – the useful one – that his mother had given to him in the bomb shelter.

How Things Turn Out

Mr Adam was walking through the streets of Berlin and entering every antique shop that was on his way. He was now on a street that had many antique shops. Some of the dealers were Jewish. They all came from Russia. Mr Adam wondered why Jews wanted to live in Germany these days, but despite much thought he did not come to a conclusion. After a few minutes he said to himself, 'Why not?' It is a country like any other country in the world. For many people the war was over, while for many others the wounds would never heal.

Mr Adam asked in every antique shop if they had any Jewish ceremonial art. In most of the shops the answer was negative. In some it was even hostile.

In this particular street where the antique shops were, he had found two Jewish objects, two Havdalah spice boxes, and he was very happy.

One of the antique dealers said that he had a very good piece of Jewish art. He had the piece at home, and if Mr Adam would come the next day he would show it to him.

'It is a very expensive piece. I paid a small fortune for it.'

'I would be interested to see it. If I like it, and the price is right, I could be a potential buyer.'

'See you tomorrow, then. *Auf wiedersehen.*'

'Goodbye.'

The next morning a big silver Hanukah lamp was on the dealer's table.

'It is from the eighteenth century. Here you can see the old Berlin silver marks.'

'You are right, but this Hanukah lamp is from the late eighteenth century.'

'Are you interested? You see, nothing is missing. Even the little oil juglet is attached, and of course its original *shamash*.'

'I can see that you are familiar with Jewish ceremonial art.'

'I am Jewish, like you. That's how I know.'

'Not every Jew knows about ceremonial pieces. Not everyone is religious.'

'Not everyone is an antique dealer, either.'

'You are right.'

'Where did you get this piece from?'

'I do not tell usually, but, if you'll believe it, I'll tell you this story.'

'Try me.'

'This Hanukah lamp was bought from a young man who was born in this country. He was brought up by a German woman. She worked very hard, at everything she could find, just to give him a good education.'

'She was not Jewish?'

'No. She was a German Christian. It was during the war, in a bomb shelter. The boy's mother left the boy with her. The boy's mother never returned. It is said that she was killed in the bombing.'

'What happened after?'

'This poor woman tried to find the family of the boy, who was her son now. She even went to a rabbi, so her son would be a Jew like any other Jew. She even learned the Jewish law. It is said that she had had a man whom she had loved, but that he was killed at the beginning of the war. When the boy was about seventeen, the Jewish community wanted to send him to Israel, to start a new life.'

'This is very interesting. Please go on.'

'When the boy was about thirteen, his new mother discovered that some of his family had lived in Basel. They went to that city and found a safe box in a Swiss bank.'

'This sounds like a real story.'

'It is a real story. In that safe box was this Hanukah lamp. There were also gold coins. When the boy was about fifteen, the mother died. She had cancer. The boy continued to live in the same house. He did not study any more. He was on the streets now. That is how he began to play. To play for money. He started to lose money, and sold whatever he found in the house. At the end, when there was nothing left for sale, he sold this Hanukah lamp to another dealer. I bought it from him.'

'You bought it with the story.'

'I am selling it with a story.'

'I'll buy it. By the way, where is the man now?'

'I do not know. Maybe wandering some place. Who knows?'

'Well, thank you very much.'

'Thank you, Mr Adam. Till next time. If I ever get something Jewish I'll keep it for you.'

Mr Adam was dusting his table when a collector entered his shop.

'Something new, Mr Adam?'

'That is a question you should never ask in an antique shop.'

'Is there something old that you have recently added to this gallery?'

'That is better. Yes, I have just brought from Germany these two Havdalah spice boxes and this magnificent silver Hanukah lamp.'

'This is magnificent. What are you asking for it?'

'This is the price. I know it is high. I paid a high price for it, but it also comes with a story.'

The collector bought the piece with the story. He was very happy. Mr Adam was quite happy too. He liked the collector, even though he liked to show off with his collection, but he was a collector for whom Mr Adam had a special feeling.

When the collector came back, after some years, and told him that his collection had been stolen, Mr Adam was very sorry; but when Mr Adam received the news that the collector had his collection back he celebrated with the collector. They had a glass of whisky together.

'I got every piece back, except for the Hanukah lamp.'

'How did you get them back?'

'Well, I have a friend who helped me in the matter. He had connections.'

'Connections with what, with whom?' Mr Adam was very excited.

'Connections with the people who stole the things, or maybe with people who knew the thieves who had my collection.'

'What did you have to do?'

'I paid. I paid a lot and got my collection back.'

Mr Adam did not know what to think. Nor did he want to think. So he said, 'You should know, my dear friend, that in police stations there are always exhibitions of stolen property. You should visit them from time to time. Maybe you'll find your Hanukah lamp.'

'Thank you, Mr Adam.'

'Have a good day.'

Six months later the collector was back in Mr Adam's shop. He was very excited. There was another customer who Mr Adam was attending to, so he had to wait. When Mr Adam wrapped the box and finished, he said to him: 'I found it! I found it!'

'You did what?'

'I found my Hanukah lamp. In the police station. It was there! You told me to go. I read in the papers every time that there was an exhibition of stolen goods. This morning my Hanukah lamp was there. I need your help.'

'What can I do for you?'

'I showed the receipt to the police inspector. The receipt you gave me when I bought the Hanukah lamp. He asked me to call you. He wants you to identify the Hanukah lamp too. He wants to be sure.'

'I'll do that with pleasure. I'll be ready in a minute!'

Mr Adam and the collector were sitting with the police inspector.

'Is this the Hanukah lamp that you sold?'

'This is the one. I brought it from Germany.'

'Are you sure?'

'Absolutely. No doubt.'

'We did not find this Hanukah lamp with the common thieves. This one we found in the home of a man who is sitting in the next room. I wonder if you know the man.'

The three men entered the room. There was somebody sitting

with his face to the wall. When he turned, Mr Adam and the collector exclaimed simultaneously:

'Gabriel!'

Man proposes, God disposes! We never know how things will turn out.

A Frame for a Painting

The apartment had been closed for over twenty years. There was a lawyer who was taking care of it and everything that was in it.

The old woman died over twenty years ago, and left no will. There were many people in her family who wanted part of her estate. The quarrels in the courtrooms did not bring anything to any member of that family, except expenses.

During those long years of dispute between the old lady's relatives, there were a few who already dropped their claims. They did not want anything any more. The lawyers' fees were now bigger than the value of the furniture and the few paintings that were in the locked apartment.

Twenty-three years passed. Five lawyers, three judges, thousands of papers and petitions; and in the apartment dust and disintegration of the objects that were there.

The last members of that family came to an agreement. After so many years, nobody wanted any object any more. Everything was to be put on sale. The new lawyer was the one who was to be in charge of the sale.

He asked many antique dealers, that day, to come and see the objects in the apartment. He asked for an offer for every piece. He also asked for an offer for the whole of the furniture and the objects.

On the wall were hanging antique maps of the Holy Land and a few prints of famous artists.

'I would like to open one of the frames of the antique maps, first to see if it is genuine, and second to see its condition.'

'You can do so. You can open every frame,' answered the lawyer.

The dealers started to open every frame of the maps. They were in a very poor condition. Some even began to crumble when they were touched. They did not open the frames of the paintings. It was not worth it. That day the lawyer sold only the furniture. He was quite happy to get rid of the objects of the apartment. He wanted to restore the apartment, to get a better price.

The next day came people from the flea market and bought all the old clothing and the old pots from the kitchen. They took a few odd pieces of china as well.

A few days later an antique dealer called the lawyer: 'I was there in the apartment the other day. I would like to buy all the maps that we saw there. They have to be very cheap because of their terrible condition.'

'Name a price.'

'I'll give you one hundred lira for all of them.'

'The frames cost more.'

'Keep the frames, but if you want to sell all the paintings as well I'll offer you three hundred lira.'

'Without the frames, I'll accept. With the frames, I'll give them to you for five hundred lira.'

'If you make it four hundred I'll take them.'

'Four hundred and fifty and they are all yours.'

'*Mazal ve berachah.*'

'What do you mean by that?'

'It is an expression between antique dealers.'

'*Mazal ve berachah.* You come first to my office and pay, and afterwards you must hurry to the apartment, because the painter is there and he is painting the walls.'

'I'll be in your office in an hour.'

The dealer was very happy. He had seen at the apartment a poster or a print of Picasso. That poster was framed, and other dealers had not noticed that there was a dedication on the left upper side of the print, which was partially covered by the thick frame. The only thing that the dealer saw were two words: '*Para misu . . .*'

If that poster really was autographed by Picasso himself, it was very valuable. If it was a lithograph, then it was worth even more. He was getting all this for nothing. He was gambling on that poster. The maps he could send to London to be restored, and he could make a good profit on them. But the poster of Picasso was a different story. If the signature was genuine he would put it up for auction in one of the big auction houses in London.

'Why did you not buy everything the last time?'

'Well, I had to find out where to restore the maps. Even now, I do not know if I am going to make a profit on the things I am buying.'

'The pictures in the frames are not worth anything?'

'No. I am just taking them for the frames.'

'I knew that the frames had some value.'

'Very little. Very little.'

The dealer rushed to the apartment and saw the painter standing on a chair. He was painting the wall – where the Picasso poster had been.

'Where is the picture that was hanging here?'

'The picture fell down. The frame is OK. It is there in the corner.'

'Where is the paper, the poster that was inside?'

'Oh, the paper? Part of it I used to clean my brushes, and the other part I am standing on. I do not want to dirty the chair. I like to keep things clean, you know.'

The dealer felt faint. He made the painter come down from the chair. There was part of the poster, all torn up into pieces. He held the pieces in his hands and started to read whatever was left:

'Mis amigos de Picas . . . '

He was sitting in the coffee house on Sheinkin Street. There were already four bottles of beer on the table. He was alone. I approached the place and saw his car parked opposite the coffee house. I saw the frames and the maps.

'Mazal Tov. You bought the maps and the old frames.'

'Yes I did. Yes.'

'Then why are you sad? You probably got them very cheaply.'

'I did. Yes, I did.'

'I was told that there was a poster of Picasso's in an old frame. I was told that it looked like an original Picasso in that frame.'

'The poster was nothing. I just bought the frame for a painting.'

48

The Rivals

The first time they met was their first day in the army. Their first fight was when both were standing in line to get their army haircut.

Jossi was born in Jerusalem, in the old city, and Uri was born in a kibbutz in the Upper Galilee.

They were rivals from the beginning. Already during basic training, the competition between Jossi and Uri was unique. It was a competition between the two boys, as there was nobody else in that unit to compete with. The others were not important. The commanding officer already knew that these two boys had something very special. Jossi and Uri had something in common. The love for the country, its history and, most of all, its archaeology.

Uri and Jossi always found time, in the field, to look for ancient coins or pottery pieces. Other soldiers saw that Jossi and Uri spoke to each other only when they had archaeological objects in their hands or, during the training, when they used to pass an archaeological site. That was the time when even the two soldiers laughed and were happy.

They were on the way to the Negev. The night of 24 December was zero hour. Army units, including also the unit of Jossi and Uri, appeared by surprise astride the Bir Asluj-Auja el Hafir highway. It was almost an impossible task, but they did it. The Egyptians were taken by surprise. They had not expected that the attack could come from any place other than the north, where the road from Beer-Sheba was.

After that it was time for the soldiers to rest. But Yossi and Uri did not rest. The area was new for them, and without saying anything to each other they started to look for archaeological objects.

'In Beer-Sheba you can find more things than here.'

'In the Galilee even more.'

'Have you ever been to Jerusalem?'

They stopped talking. It was clear that a new fight was on the way. They went different ways; Jossi went to the right and Uri went to the left.

Two hours later, Yossi found a cave. The entrance was very small and he could not get in. He made a bigger hole, and after a while he was in the cave. It was a very big cave. It was an ancient tomb. He found very big pottery jars and there were traces of bones. There was also the complete skeleton of an animal. He saw that the cave had a continuation and so he started to walk. He saw more pottery jars, and his excitement grew with every step. It was the biggest discovery of his life. He had never seen a complete tomb. Everything was there. Just as he had seen in his books, or in an archaeological museum.

When Jossi entered the third room of the cave he saw Uri. He was standing there. 'How did you get in? This is my cave.'

'I could ask you the same question. This is my cave.'

The two young men started to fight like little boys. It was a bad fight and they hurt each other. There was no winner. An hour later, both were still sitting in the cave. They decided that they would leave the cave as it was, and that they would not take any antiquities until the war was over. They were partners and co-owners of that big tomb and all that was in it.

The War of Independence was over. The state of Israel was a reality. Uri and Jossi met again when they were called for their army service. They were in the reserve service now. The day they met, they embraced like brothers, All the soldiers in their unit were happy to see each other again.

'You should see the archaeological objects I added this year to my collection. You would die. You have never seen anything like it.'

'You are always so modest. Modesty was always your biggest virtue.'

'That is because you have not seen my collection.'

'You have not seen mine either, and I can assure you that mine is much bigger than yours. I now have objects from almost every period.'

'That is because you buy antiquities. I am a kibbutznik. I do not have money. I excavate.'

Uri and Jossi were like little children again. They almost started to fight.

'Did you go to the cave?'

'No, did you?'

'No. I think we should go together.'

'I hope that nobody else has discovered it since.'

'After we finish with the army service, we'll take the command car and pick everything up.'

They found the cave with no problem. The same stones that they had put in the two entrances were still there. They entered. Everything was there. Uri and Jossi started to make an inventory of the artifacts.

'Here are six jars. Let's throw a coin to see who chooses first.'

'Tails!'

For about two hours they worked together, and it was then clear that each of the young men had an archaeological collection of ancient pottery of the Holy Land.

Years passed, and every year they met on their army service. That was also the time when they went together to find antiquities. Many times there were fights between them, like the first fight they had.

That year they decided to cross the border to Jordan.

'We have to be very careful. The Jordanian Arab legion is nearby.'

'If you are afraid, you can stay. I'll go. I'll tell you afterwards how it is over there.'

'Shut up! Or I'll hit you.'

'OK, let's go.'

'You go to the right and I'll go to the left.'

The shooting started after half an hour. Yossi knew that something was wrong. He crossed the border, back to Israel, and went to his army camp. He asked everyone if they had seen Uri, but the answers were negative. He was worried.

'I must go and find him.' All the other soldiers said that it was a crazy idea. The Arab legion could be anywhere. He should stay. Uri was a good soldier and he knew what to do.

It was still dark in the early morning. Jossi filled his canteen with water, checked his rifle, and started to walk to the border. He crossed the border and climbed up, next to an Arab village called Sicka. That was the direction that Uri had taken. After two hours of searching, he found no trace of him. He whistled all the time, so that if Uri was nearby he could hear him. He was now at the place where many caves were. The sun was up. Jossi was now in great danger too.

'I'll try once more. I'll whistle once more.'

He heard a whistle from a cave. Jossi approached the cave, and saw traces of blood at the entrance.

'Uri! Uri! Are you all right?!'

'I am here. I cannot walk. I am wounded.'

'Stay where you are. I'll come over.'

Uri was shot in his legs. Jossi took his first aid kit and helped his friend.

'We'll have to wait till dark again.'

'That is a long time. It is very painful.'

'I have only two morphine shots. I'll give you one now; the second in the evening, when I'll take you home.'

'Thanks, Jossi, for coming.'

'I did not come for you. I just wanted to make sure that you wouldn't get more antiquities. I mean more than me,' he answered, smiling.

'You must be crazy.'

'To get shot for a few pottery jars?'

'To get shot for loving the living Bible.'

'I think we are both crazy.'

'Have you seen what is in this cave?'

'Who cares!'

'I do.'

Jossi looked around. There were ossuaries all over. Ancient jars were lying next to them.

'It is a tomb.'

'It looks as if it's from the Second Temple period.'

'One day we'll come back. It is our cave.'

'Yes. It is ours.'

The day passed very slowly. Uri was in great pain. Jossi comforted him as well as he could. When it started to get dark, Jossi carried Uri back to the border. The shooting started again. They had been seen by the Jordanian soldiers. Jossi ran all the way. The Israeli side opened fire to protect them. Jossi crossed the border. They were safely home. Both were injured. They were both in hospital now.

'Because of you, I am here.'

'You are an idiot. You should not have come.'

'You are the idiot.'

Nurses and doctors had to run to the room. Jossi and Uri were fighting again. Everybody thought that they were rivals.

Many years later, they found themselves in the cave, the same cave in which they were together the last time. But this time they were not alone. They had brought their children along too. It was difficult for Uri and Jossi to stop their children from fighting among themselves. A new generation of friendly rivals had begun.

The Letter

The old man lived in a very small apartment, which was on a street that once was in the centre of Tel-Aviv.

Every morning he had his tea at Nahum's coffee house on Rambam Street. He loved to talk about the old times, when a collector was a collector. The times when collectors had no money and built their collections with knowledge, intuition, love and time.

Years ago he had been the porter of the Bezalel Museum in Jerusalem. It was part of the Bezalel Art School, before it was transferred to what today is the Israel Museum.

He lived in a little two-room apartment that was located in the cellar of the house. He had been given the apartment as he was the caretaker of the house. He had no family and was a very strange person indeed. So strange that he did not have electricity or water in his apartment.

His two rooms were like a little museum. Old pictures, jars, some archaeological objects, old books, porcelain, etc. He had everything in his collection. He always used to say about his collection that it was an international one. He did not care where the pieces were from, or what they were. The important thing was that he loved them. He used to fall in love with an antique, and as long as he loved it it was there. He took care of it, and used to sit for hours just looking at the piece, until it was dark. He went to sleep when the birds went to sleep. He used to get up in the morning when the birds announced the new day.

The day that he decided that he did not love a piece any more, that was the day that the object was to be exchanged for a new love. He used to go to all the dealers and knew exactly what he wanted. He also knew what the dealers were looking for. He needed very little money to live. He had his special hours when and where to go, so he would be invited for a cup of tea and maybe, if he was lucky, he would get a sandwich as well.

Nahum knew the man very well, and it was very rare that Nahum charged the man for the tea.

'You are late today, Mr Shwartz. It is already seven thirty. Your tea is getting cold.'

It was not true, but that was the way that Nahum's greetings were in the early morning.

Shwartz didn't want to drink his tea every day at Nahum's expense, though. So he used to walk outside the coffee shop until he was invited in. If Garbash was the first to come, he usually invited Shwartz for breakfast, and if I was the first, then Shwartz was my guest.

Shwartz had also a collection of letters. It was a small collection, but every dealer wanted to buy it. The collection had letters of Theodor Herzel, Ben-Gurion, Jabotinsky, Bialik, Beh-Yehuda and so on.

When he exchanged his antiques for the letters, people were not very interested in them, but after the creation of the state of Israel everything that had to do with Jewish personalities became very important. At first they were very cheap, and that was the reason why Shwartz had them in his collection.

Many dealers used to invite Shwartz for a coffee or a meal, but what they really wanted was to buy the letters he possessed. He always used to say, 'If I ever need the money, I am going to sell. Now, I do not need any money.'

'But you can buy yourself a new suit.'

'I am not invited to a wedding, so I do not need a new suit.'

'If you would be invited to a wedding, would you buy a new suit?'

'I would not go to the wedding.'

That was the end of the conversation, which meant that he was not selling.

One morning at Nahum's place, Shwartz told me that he was considering selling one of the Herzel letters he had. 'I think I am going to need some money for the next months to come.'

'Which letter do you want to sell?'

'I think the introduction letter.'

'How much do you want for it?'

'I am going to find out how much it is worth, and then I'll tell you.'

'You don't know how much you want for it?'

'I do, but I want to see first how much I am going to get from other antique dealers.'

'In any case, I'll offer you fifty lira more than the best offer you can get.'

'How would you know that I am telling the truth, I mean about the offer?'

'I do not see any reason why you would lie to me.'

Months later, though I saw Shwartz almost every day, he said, 'I am willing to sell now.'

'In all these months you did not need money?'

'It is not that. Now I am selling. Are you still interested?'

'Yes.'

'This is the highest price I have been offered for the letter. Are you still offering fifty lira more?'

'Yes.'

'I'll bring it in tomorrow morning.'

The next morning I bought the letter. It was not a very important one, but it was Herzel's, and that was important. I had had the letter for some months when Shwartz entered the gallery.

'I would like to buy the letter back. Ever since I sold the letter, I have the feeling that I did something wrong. That I should not have sold it.'

'Why is that?'

'I do not know. I am so afraid that you might sell it to a collector in America or Europe, and actually it should be here, in Israel.'

'I do not know what to say. A deal is a deal.'

'Really, I have known you for so many years, please try to help me.'

'I do not even know, did you get a bigger offer?'

'Oh no! I would not do something like that. I just want my letter back.'

'I am going to think it over. I'll let you know.'

'This letter was part of a collection of letters I had. Now I have this terrible feeling that I destroyed something. The same feeling I had when thieves broke into my home. Not only did they steal art objects from me, they destroyed my dream. They destroyed my collection.'

'You can have your letter back, for the same price.'

'I do not have all the money. I have most of it. I'll give you something else for the difference.'

'It is all right. We won't have to go to the rabbi for it.'

Two months later, I heard that Shwartz was in the hospital. I went to see him. He was very ill. He lay there very still, without a movement. It was the first time I saw him without his thick glasses. I talked to him for a while. It seemed that he was not very interested in the conversation. The nurse came into the room. I was supposed to leave. I stood up and said goodbye to him. He raised his head and said, 'Thank you.'

'I'll be back. I'll come to see you again.'

'Thank you for the letter.'

Three weeks later Shwartz died. He left his complete collection to the city of Tel-Aviv.

The Faithless

He was an antique dealer in Jerusalem. Always very well-dressed. It was early in the morning. He had his coffee and got dressed. He took a new snow-white shirt from the wardrobe and started to brush, very carefully, his black suit. He was ready now for his morning prayers.

He had his prayer strings wound around his head and round his left arm. That was the way it had to be, so that his heart beat against the capsule containing the Creed. He always stood in the same place that he had been doing for so many years. He was saying the 'eighteen prayers', with his face towards the east, the direction of the temple, his feet together, always in the same position, as the ritual prescribes.

'Oh, my God. Guard my tongue from evil and my lips from speaking guile, and to such as curse me let my soul be dumb. Yea, let my soul be unto all as the dust . . .'

While he was praying, he was surprised how fast he could pray. He always prayed at top speed to prevent other thoughts from coming to his mind. He was afraid that the devil would distract him from the prayer, so he used to hold his *talis* (prayer shawl) very tightly, very tightly indeed.

That day he was early in his shop. He did not have to go to the bank and he did not have any other appointments. A Hungarian antique dealer entered the shop: 'I think that I have something very interesting for you. I think that it is something that you have been looking for for a long time.'

213

'Show me.'

'This is a very rare eighteenth-century *Ketubah**.'

'Let me see . . . yes, the date is 1772. From Ancona, Italy.'

'I knew that you were interested. Isn't it beautiful?'

'It is.'

'It's not very expensive either.'

'How much are you asking for it?'

'Half the usual price, and there are more.'

'Half the price? Why? Is there something wrong?'

'It is a fake. I know the man who makes them. He is a professional. Nobody can tell the difference between a real one and this one.'

'That is true. I cannot see anything that might show that this is a fake. The old parchment, the old ink . . . even the old tempera colours.'

'I'll tell you. He is an artist who knows exactly the way they made the real ones in their time. He studied the subject and he is a real professional.'

'How many more *Ketubahs* do you have?'

'Another twenty-five.'

'It is very tempting.'

'The demand for Italian *Ketubahs*, in particular, is so great that it would be very easy for you to sell them.'

'But real experts could somehow find out.'

'Three experts, from three different museums, have already bought them, so if one of them is going to be asked there will be only one answer. That they are real because they are similar to the ones they bought. You understand?'

'Yes, but . . .'

'This is going to be a very good moneymaker. There are about five hundred collectors of Jewish ceremonial art who would buy a piece like this for their collection. If you sell five hundred of these, during a few years, you are rich.'

'We should discuss a better price for each, if I am going to buy the whole collection.'

'You mean all the twenty-six marriage contracts?'

'Yes.'

The two antique dealers discussed for over an hour, but they

---

* A Jewish marriage contract, always written in Aramaic.

came to an agreement. The deal was sealed, and it seemed that they were pleased.

It was evening, and he was praying again, in the same place that he had done for many years.

'Thou sustainest the living with loving kindness, thou quickenest the dead with great mercy, supportest the falling, healest the sick, loosest the bound.'

Again he finished his prayers very quickly and started to make a list of the people to whom he would send photographs of the *Ketubahs*. He worked till very late and he had his list ready.

After his morning prayers he went to his friend, the photographer, and made an appointment to photograph all the twenty-six *Ketubahs*. The next day the photographs were ready. He had finished writing the introduction letters, and did not forget to mention the names of the museums, and their curators, which had similar marriage contracts.

The orders came very fast. Every time he saw an envelope from America or Europe, he knew that a cheque was inside. He sold each *Ketubah* for a very high price, even though it was always a bit less than the price at the last auction.

A few weeks later he had none left. He started to look for the address of the Hungarian and could not find it. He looked in every drawer, he checked every paper. No address. He rushed home and started to look all over. Nothing. 'Such a good business, and now I cannot find his address,' he thought.

He went through all the telephone books, and tried to remember the last name of the Hungarian dealer. He even tried a few who he thought might be his man, but no luck. That night he did not sleep well. He had a bad dream. His late father appeared in his dream: 'You have done something wrong. Because of you, I cannot rest in peace. You have to return the money to the people you have cheated. I have no rest because of you.'

He woke up. He was all wet. He was sweating and he felt freezing cold. 'I might be ill. It is just a dream. It is nothing.'

The next morning he prayed again: 'We give thanks unto Thee, for Thou are the Lord, our God, and the God of our fathers.' When he said 'fathers' he remembered his dream again. He did not want to think about it, so he continued very fast, '. . . for ever

215

and ever, Thou are the rock of our lives, the shield of our salvation.'

It was very early, and he was sitting in his shop. What was he to do? He still wanted to find the address of the Hungarian antique dealer. Every time he started to look in a certain place, he remembered his dream. He stopped looking for the missing address.

He finished his evening prayers, had something to eat, and went straight to bed. He had slept badly the night before. He needed rest. But that night he had the same dream. His late father was there again. He said to him the same thing as he had said the night before. He woke up in a panic. He started to scream. All the members of the family came to calm him down.

The dream recurred every night now. He was afraid to go to sleep. He went to a *chacham*, a wise man, for advice. He only told the *chacham* half of the truth. He did not tell the story of the *Ketubahs*. He was known as a very reputable antique dealer. The wise man told him that if a dead person appears in a dream, some of his everyday deeds were wrong, and only he was the one who actually knew what was wrong.

Yom Kippur was coming soon. He was afraid. He had made a small fortune out of the *Ketubahs* and he was unhappy.

That night he had the dream again. His father appeared and said to him: 'Yom Kippur is in one month. You cannot make peace with God if you have not made peace with your fellow man. I cannot rest in peace.'

He woke up, soaked in sweat again. He dressed and went to the shop. It was a very dark night. He went directly to the list of the customers to whom he had sold the marriage contracts, the fake *Ketubahs*. He wrote everyone a letter of apology, stating that he thought that the *Ketubah* that each had purchased had to be checked again. He was the first at the post office the next morning and sent every letter by special delivery. He offered to refund, to the last cent, every purchase, and he even offered some interest on the money he had received and had held all that time. When he dropped the last letter in the box, he felt relieved. He had remembered that he had not prayed that morning. He rushed home.

He had his prayer strings wound round his head and round his left arm, so that his heart beat against the capsule containing the Creed, and he stood there. The same place he always stood, twice every day.

He remembered what his late father had told him: 'At the end of the prayer, you have to go three steps backwards. To make peace with your God. Why three? Because the first one everybody would do. That is simple. The second means that you really mean it, and that is difficult. The third step is the step which you take because you meant it, and that is the most difficult one. You cannot make peace with God if you have not made peace with your friend. To make peace with your friend you have to go back three steps too.'

'He who makes peace in his high place, may he make peace for us and for all Israel, and say ye amen.' He prayed, stepped back three steps as is prescribed, took three steps forward, and bowed from the waist. He said again: 'Amen.'